Better Homes and Gardens®

Four Seasons
CROSS-STITCH

© Copyright 1990 by Meredith Corporation, Des Moines, Iowa.
All Rights Reserved. Printed in the United States of America.
First Edition. Second Printing, 1991.
Library of Congress Catalog Card Number: 89-82440
ISBN: 0-696-01875-6

BETTER HOMES AND GARDENS® BOOKS

Editor: Gerald M. Knox
Art Director: Ernest Shelton
Managing Editor: David A. Kirchner
Project Editors: James D. Blume, Marsha Jahns
Project Managers: Liz Anderson,
    Jennifer Speer Ramundt, Angela K. Renkoski

Crafts Editor: Sara Jane Treinen
Senior Crafts Editors: Beverly Rivers, Patricia Wilens
Associate Crafts Editor: Nancy Reames

Associate Art Directors: Neoma Thomas,
    Linda Ford Vermie, Randall Yontz
Assistant Art Directors: Lynda Haupert,
    Harijs Priekulis, Tom Wegner
Graphic Designers: Mary Schlueter Bendgen,
    Michael Burns, Mick Schnepf
Art Production: Director, John Berg;
    Associate, Joe Heuer;
    Office Manager, Michaela Lester

President, Book Group: Jeramy Lanigan
Vice President, Retail Marketing: Jamie L. Martin
Vice President, Administrative Services: Rick Rundall

BETTER HOMES AND GARDENS® MAGAZINE
President, Magazine Group: James A. Autry
Editorial Director: Doris Eby

MEREDITH CORPORATION OFFICERS
Chairman of the Executive Committee: E. T. Meredith III
Chairman of the Board: Robert A. Burnett
President and Chief Executive Officer: Jack D. Rehm

Four-Seasons Cross-Stitch
Editor: Beverly Rivers
Project Manager: Liz Anderson
Graphic Designer: Michael Burns
Electronic Text Processor: Alice Bauman
Contributing Writers: Carol McGarvey,
    Sharon L. Novotne O'Keefe
Contributing Illustrator: Andy Haluska

Cover project: See pages 8 and 9.

From the crisp clarity of a winter land-scape to the radiant beauty of a summer garden, the changing of the seasons offers a medley of color and pattern for the avid and the beginning needleworker.

Our collection of cross-stitch designs celebrates the natural beauty and festivities of each season from New Year's to Christmas.

Four-Seasons Cross-Stitch *showcases 86 projects to make each of your holidays and special events unforgettable. We hope you'll eagerly anticipate your favorite days of the four seasons as you move from chapter to chapter creating beautiful linens, samplers, wall hangings, dresser boxes, clothing, and much more.*

CONTENTS

CELEBRATIONS OF THE SEASONS   6

A Wonderland of Gifts for
WINTER CRAFTING   22

FAVORITE DAYS OF WINTER   38

Nature's Finest Gifts
SPRINGTIME'S BLESSINGS   64

FAVORITE DAYS OF SPRING   84

A Year-Round Event
ROMANTIC NOTIONS FOR A PASTEL WEDDING   108

For Sunny Days
SUMMER PLEASURES   116

FAVORITE DAYS OF SUMMER   138

A Year-Round Event
PRECIOUS GIFTS TO WELCOME BABY   152

Nature's Vibrant Colors
AUTUMN'S SPLENDOR   162

FAVORITE DAYS OF AUTUMN   176

Merry Christmas to All
RECOLLECTIONS OF CHRISTMASTIME AT HOME   192

TIPS AND TECHNIQUES   216

ACKNOWLEDGMENTS   220

INDEX   222

Recapture the merriment of a frosty winter morning when your family dashed out into the fresh-fallen snow to make a memory, complete with stovepipe hat and carrot nose.

Richly layered stitching brings this heartwarming design to life. Worked on 14-count Aida cloth, the unframed portrait measures 7¼x8½ inches. The cross-stitching is embellished with fanciful detailing, from the snowman's sparkles to the daughter's ringlets. How-to instructions begin on page 14.

CELEBRATIONS OF THE SEASONS

A simple family pleasure and the special decorative stitches seen in this charming spring scene make this cross-stitch so realistic you can almost feel the warm spring breezes that have sent these colorful kites soaring. Dozens of details add texture and dimension to this 7½x9-inch stitchery and invite you to show off your needlecrafts and stitching repertoire.

To guide you through the subtle shadings, this and the other seasonal scenes each have a separate color key, stitching chart, and materials list. Pattern and instructions for this design begin on page 16.

Many a childhood reverie and family album are filled with images of fun-filled summer days at the seashore, crafting medieval fantasies with turrets of glistening sand. Strands of gold metallic floss create the sparkles on this sand castle and tiny lazy daisy stitches detail the sand dollars.

The finished stitchery is 6½x8¼ inches unframed. How-to instructions begin on page 18.

 *A bounteous fall finds our old-fashioned clan in the orchard, harvesting Mother Nature's ruby red riches and sharing love and laughter.*

Creatively framing the cross-stitch "snapshots" is part of the fun. Charming apple pickers are showcased here in a wooden country frame with a heart cutout at the top. Mat and finish all four pieces the same, or suit each season with a different new or antique frame.

Instructions and patterns for this project begin on page 20.

WINTER FAMILY SCENE

Shown on pages 6 and 7.
Finished size of stitchery is approximately 7¼x8½ inches.
Design is 103x117 stitches.

MATERIALS
14x15-inch piece of 14-count Aida cloth
DMC embroidery floss in colors listed on the color key; number of skeins required appears in parentheses
Tapestry needle
Embroidery hoop

INSTRUCTIONS
Carefully read all instructions before you begin to stitch. The chart for the design is on page 15.

Hem or tape the raw edges of the fabric to prevent threads from raveling.

Locate the center of the fabric and the center of the chart; begin stitching here. (Arrows mark the centers on the pattern.)

Use two strands of floss to work the cross-stitches over one square of the Aida cloth.

Work one cross-stitch for each symbol on the chart.

Decorative Stitches
When the foundation cross-stitching is complete, work the following decorative stitches for added dimension (see page 216 for stitch diagrams):

DUPLICATE CROSS-STITCHES (indicated by special red symbols on color key): The entire body of the snowman is worked with white floss and shaded with No. 415 light gray. Work a second set of cross-stitches over the first using one strand of metallic silver to add sparkles.

BACKSTITCHES (solid red outlines on chart): For pupils of mother's, daughter's, father's, and son's eyes, work short backstitches using one strand of No. 3371 black-brown.

Use one strand of black-brown to define the crosshatch lines on the four pinecones (at the feet of the two children) and to backstitch the mother's, daughter's, father's, and son's facial features. Use black-brown for outlining trees, snowman, and all clothing.

STRAIGHT STITCHES (shown as long solid red lines on chart): For mother's hair and daughter's bangs, work straight stitches using one strand *each* of No. 435 light chestnut and No. 433 dark chestnut together.

For father's mustache and branches of pine boughs (at daughter's feet), work straight stitches using one strand *each* of No. 838 dark brown and No. 3371 black-brown together.

For needles on pine bough, work straight stitches using one strand *each* of No. 986 light green and No. 890 dark green together.

For son's hair, work straight stitches using one strand *each* of No. 676 medium gold and No. 838 dark brown together.

For snowman's mouth, work straight stitches using one strand *each* of No. 815 medium red and No. 814 dark red together. For fringe on snowman's scarf, work straight stitches using one strand *each* of No. 680 dark gold and No. 814 dark red together.

For buckles on son's boot, work straight stitches using one strand *each* of No. 310 black and metallic silver together.

WRAPPED STITCHES (red spirals on chart): *Note:* To make wrapped stitches, first work straight stitches and then wrap those stitches loosely with the same thread.

For mother's bangs and daughter's ringlets, work wrapped stitches using one strand *each* of No. 435 light chestnut and No. 433 dark chestnut together.

FRENCH KNOTS: For father's hair, work random French knots over cross-stitches using one strand of No. 838 dark brown and No. 3371 black-brown together.

Make two French not buttons on both of daughter's boots using two strands of No. 3371 black-brown.

For lace on top of mother's collar, work row of French knots using two strands of white.

For knots on the fringe of the snowman's scarf, work French knots using one strand *each* of No. 680 dark gold and No. 814 dark red.

TO FINISH: Lightly press finished stitchery on back side. Frame as desired.

COLOR KEY
⊠ **White (1)**
▦ **Black 310 (1)**
✳ **Dark Gray 413 (1)**
☐ **Light Gray 415 (1)**
■ **Dark Flesh 950 (1)**
▣ **Light Flesh 948 (1)**
▶ **Dark Gold 680 (1)**
⊠ **Medium Gold 676 (1)**
◣ **Black-Brown 3371 (1)**
⊞ **Dark Brown 838 (1)**
— **Light Brown 840 (1)**
▨ **Dark Chestnut 433 (1)**
◥ **Light Chestnut 435 (1)**
▦ **Dark Green 890 (1)**
◎ **Light Green 986 (2)**
▨ **Dark Olive 935 (1)**
⊠ **Medium Olive 937 (1)**
◪ **Dark Red 814 (1)**
⊠ **Medium Red 815 (1)**
◣ **Medium Pink 604 (1)**
● **Dark Navy 823 (1)**
▣ **Light Navy 824 (1)**
☐ **Dark Rust 919 (1)**
⊞ **Light Rust 921 (1)**
⊠ **Metallic Silver over White**

WINTER FAMILY SCENE

1 Square = 1 Stitch

15

SPRING FAMILY SCENE

1 Square = 1 Stitch

SPRING FAMILY SCENE

Shown on pages 8 and 9.
Finished size of stitchery is 7½x9 inches.
Design is 107x127 stitches.

MATERIALS

13½x15-inch piece of 14-count Aida cloth
One skein of DMC embroidery floss in colors listed on the color key
Tapestry needle; embroidery hoop

COLOR KEY

- ▣ Dark Gray 413
- ◙ Medium Gray 414
- ⊠ Light Gray 415
- ▣ Dark Flesh 754
- ⊕ Light Flesh 948
- ▶ Dark Gold 680
- ⊠ Medium Gold 676
- ● Dark Chestnut 433
- ◥ Light Chestnut 435
- ⊞ Black-Brown 3371
- ◥ Dark Brown 838
- – Light Brown 840
- ✳ Sand 842
- ▥ Forest Green 890
- ▨ Dark Green 3346
- ⊠ Medium Green 3347
- ⊠ Light Green 3348
- ◿ Dark Yellow 743
- ⊠ Light Yellow 745
- ▨ Dark Coral 3706
- ⊡ Light Coral 3708
- ⊞ Dark Pink 603
- ⊡ Light Pink 605
- □ Dark Lavender 208
- ▷ Light Lavender 210
- ◥ Dark Blue 825
- ⊟ Light Blue 826
- ⊠ Light Orchid 3608
- ◪ Dark Orchid 3607
- ◩ White
- ▣ Tan 407
- ▨ Light Tan 950
- ◉ 605 over 603
- ▨ 605 over 3607
- Light Gold 677

INSTRUCTIONS

The chart for the design is on page 16.
Carefully read General Instructions on page 14 before you begin to stitch.

Decorative Stitches

When foundation cross-stitching is complete, work the following decorative stitches (see page 216 for stitch diagrams):

DUPLICATE CROSS-STITCHES (indicated by special red symbols on the color key): Work apple blossoms on tree using two strands of No. 603 dark pink and No. 3607 dark orchid as indicated on color key. Then work a second set of stitches over the first ones using one strand of No. 605 light pink.

BACKSTITCHES (solid red outlines on chart): For crosshatch marks on mother's dress and ribbing on daughter's stockings, work backstitches using one strand of No. 208 dark lavender.

For ribbing on son's stockings, work backstitches using one strand of No. 413 dark gray. For eye pupils, work backstitches using one strand of No. 3371 black-brown.

For kite strings; mother's, daughter's, father's, and son's facial features; and all remaining outlining, work backstitches using one strand of No. 3371 black-brown.

STRAIGHT STITCHES (long solid red lines on chart): For mother's hair and daughter's bangs, work straight stitches using one strand *each* of No. 435 light chestnut and No. 433 dark chestnut together. For father's mustache, work straight stitches using one strand *each* of No. 838 dark brown and No. 3371 black-brown together.

For son's hair, work straight stitches using one strand *each* of No. 677 light gold and No. 680 dark gold together. For ribbon on daughter's hat, work straight stitches using one strand *each* of No. 3348 light green and No. 3347 medium green together.

WRAPPED STITCHES (red spirals on chart): *Note:* To make wrapped stitches, first work long straight stitches and then wrap loosely with the same thread.

For mother's bangs and daughter's ringlets, work wrapped stitches using one strand *each* of No. 435 light chestnut and No. 433 dark chestnut together.

DAISY STITCHES (red loops on chart): For bow on hat, work daisy stitches using one strand *each* of No. 3348 light green and No. 3347 medium green together.

For bows on kites, work daisy stitches using one strand *each* of No. 745 light yellow and No. 743 dark yellow together on the yellow kite; one strand *each* of No. 605 light pink and No. 603 dark pink on the pink kite; one strand *each* of No. 826 light blue and No. 825 dark blue on the blue kite; and one strand *each* of No. 210 light lavender and No. 208 dark lavender on the lavender kite.

ROSEBUDS (large open red ovals on chart): *Note:* To make rosebuds, work two straight stitches side by side; add a French knot between them. For each flower on daughter's hat, work a rosebud using two strands of No. 3608 light orchid for the straight stitches and two strands of No. 3607 dark orchid for the French knot.

FRENCH KNOTS: For father's hair, work random French knots over cross-stitches using one strand *each* of No. 838 dark brown and No. 3371 black-brown.

Add French knots for lace along mother's dress hem, collar, and cuffs, and edge of each layer of back ruffles, using one strand of No. 745 light yellow.

For buttons down front of father's shirt, work French knots using one strand of white.

For lilies of the valley in the grass, mix random French knots over cross-stitches among flowers using two strands of white.

TO FINISH: Lightly press finished stitchery on back side. Frame as desired.

SUMMER FAMILY SCENE

Shown on pages 10 and 11.
Finished size of stitchery is 6½x8¼ inches.
Design is 91x116 stitches.

MATERIALS
12½x14-inch piece of 14-count Aida cloth
One skein of DMC embroidery floss in colors listed on the color key
Tapestry needle
Embroidery hoop

INSTRUCTIONS
Carefully read all instructions before you begin to stitch. The chart for the design is on page 19.

Hem or tape the raw edges of the fabric to prevent threads from raveling. Use two strands of floss to work the cross-stitches over one thread of the Aida cloth.

Locate the center of the fabric and the center of the chart (see arrows on chart); begin stitching here. Work one cross-stitch for each symbol on the chart.

Decorative Stitches
When foundation cross-stitching is complete, work decorative stitches as follows (see page 216 for stitch diagrams):

DUPLICATE CROSS-STITCHES (indicated by special red symbols on the color key): When stitching the sand castle, work the background colors first. After that stitching is complete, place a second cross-stitch over the first, using one strand of metallic gold to add sparkle.

When working the starfish, first work the starfish with No. 676 medium gold and No. 680 dark gold, then work a second set of cross-stitches over the first using one strand of No. 433 dark chestnut.

BACKSTITCHES (solid red outlines on chart): For pupils of mother's and father's eyes and for daughter's and son's eyelashes, work short backstitches using one strand of No. 3371 black-brown.

For mother's, daughter's, father's, and son's facial features, and all outlining, work backstitches using one strand of black-brown.

STRAIGHT STITCHES (shown as long solid red lines on chart): For mother's hair and daughter's bangs, work straight stitches using one strand *each* of No. 435 light chestnut and No. 433 dark chestnut together.

For father's mustache, work straight stitches using one strand *each* of No. 838 dark brown and No. 3371 black-brown together. For son's hair, work straight stitches using one strand *each* of No. 677 light gold and No. 838 dark brown together.

WRAPPED STITCHES (red spirals on chart): *Note:* To make wrapped stitches, first work long straight stitches and then wrap those stitches loosely with the same thread.

For mother's and daughter's ringlets, work wrapped stitches using one strand *each* of No. 435 light chestnut and No. 433 dark chestnut together.

DAISY STITCHES (red loops on chart): For design on the sand dollars, work daisy stitches using one strand of No. 3371 black-brown.

FRENCH KNOTS: For father's hair, work random French knots over cross-stitches using one strand of No. 838 dark brown and No. 3371 black-brown together.

For pebbles at base of sand castle, work an equal number of interspersed French knots randomly on the ground using one strand of No. 613 light tan and No. 610 dark tan together; No. 677 light gold and No. 680 dark gold together; and No. 415 light gray and No. 413 dark gray together.

Using one strand of No. 612 medium tan, work one French knot over each white cross-stitch on windows and door.

TO FINISH: Lightly press finished stitchery on back side. Frame as desired.

COLOR KEY
◩ White
◼ Dark Gray 413
◎ Medium Gray 414
⊠ Light Gray 415
▦ Dark Flesh 950
⊕ Light Flesh 948
▶ Dark Gold 680
⊞ Medium Gold 676
◲ Black-Brown 3371
⊡ Dark Brown 838
◉ Dark Chestnut 433
◤ Light Chestnut 435
✳ Dark Teal 943
▯ Light Teal 959
▣ Dark Tan 610
⊟ Medium Tan 612
⊡ Dark Pink 602
⊠ Medium Pink 604
◿ Medium Red 815
◗ Light Red 817
⊟ Dark Blue 796
⊡ Light Blue 798
⊠ Dark Orange 947
⊡ Light Orange 740
◎ 433 over 680
⊠ 433 over 676
⊡ Gold Metallic over 610
⊡ Gold Metallic over 612
Light Gold 677
Light Tan 613

SUMMER FAMILY SCENE

1 Square = 1 Stitch

AUTUMN FAMILY SCENE

Shown on pages 12 and 13.
Finished size of stitchery is 7¼x8¾ inches.
Design is 102x122 stitches.

MATERIALS

13½x15-inch piece of 14-count Aida cloth
One skein of DMC embroidery floss in colors listed on the color key
Tapestry needle
Embroidery hoop

INSTRUCTIONS

Carefully read all instructions before you begin to stitch. The chart for the design is on page 21.

Hem or tape the raw edges of the fabric to prevent threads from raveling.

Use two strands of floss to work the cross-stitches over one fabric square.

Locate the center of the fabric and the center of the chart (see arrows on pattern); begin stitching here. Work one cross-stitch for each symbol on the chart.

Decorative Stitches

When the foundation cross-stitching is complete, work the following decorative stitches (see page 216 for stitch diagrams):

BACKSTITCHES (solid red outlines on chart): For ribbing on son's stockings, work backstitches using one strand of No. 413 dark gray.

For ribbing on daughter's stockings, work backstitches using one strand of No. 840 light brown.

For ribbing on son's sweater cuffs and at waist and for cross-hatching on son's knickers, work backstitches using one strand of No. 838 dark brown.

For pupils of mother's, father's, and son's eyes and for daughter's eyelashes, work short backstitches using two strands of No. 3371 black-brown.

For mother's, daughter's, father's, and son's facial features and all outlining, work backstitches using one strand of No. 3371 black-brown.

STRAIGHT STITCHES (long solid red lines on chart): For mother's bangs and daughter's bangs and braid, work straight stitches using one strand *each* of No. 435 light chestnut and No. 433 dark chestnut together.

For the son's hair, work straight stitches using one strand *each* of No. 677 light gold and No. 838 dark brown together.

For the father's mustache, work straight stitches using one strand *each* of No. 838 dark brown and No. 3371 black-brown together.

WRAPPED STITCHES (red spirals on chart): *Note:* To make wrapped stitches, first work straight stitches and then wrap those stitches loosely with the same thread.

For mother's ringlets, work wrapped stitches using one strand *each* of No. 435 light chestnut and No. 433 dark chestnut together.

FRENCH KNOTS: For the father's hair, work random French knots over cross-stitches using one strand *each* of No. 838 dark brown and No. 3371 black-brown floss together.

Make five French knots for buttons on mother's blouse using two strands of white. Make a row of French knots along the bottom of daughter's petticoat using two strands of white.

Make four French knot buttons on father's shirt front and one on the shirt cuff using two strands of No. 414 medium gray.

TO FINISH: Lightly press finished stitchery on back side. Frame as desired.

COLOR KEY

- ◨ White
- ◻ Ecru
- ✳ Dark Ecru 3033
- ◼ Dark Gray 413
- ◎ Medium Gray 414
- ⊠ Light Gray 415
- ▥ Dark Flesh 950
- ⊕ Light Flesh 948
- ▸ Dark Gold 680
- ⊠ Medium Gold 676
- ⊞ Light Gold 677
- ◉ Dark Chestnut 433
- ◩ Light Chestnut 435
- ◩ Black-Brown 3371
- ⊞ Dark Brown 838
- ⊟ Light Brown 840
- ▦ Dark Olive 935
- ◗ Medium Olive 937
- ⊠ Light Olive 471
- ▤ Medium Red 815
- ⊿ Light Red 817
- ⊠ Medium Pink 604
- ◥ Dark Blue 311
- ⊡ Light Blue 312
- ▧ Dark Rust 919
- ⊡ Light Rust 921

AUTUMN FAMILY SCENE

1 Square = 1 Stitch

A Wonderland of Gifts for

WINTER CRAFTING

Patterned after samplers handed down by our ancestors, the projects in this chapter duplicate the harmonious combination of alphabets and numbers shown in antique samplers and reflect an intriguing representation of each stitcher's interests.

The sampler at *right* is a glorious way to mark the changing of the seasons. Corner motifs are autumn leaves for fall, tulips and daffodils for spring, a bouquet of daisies for summer, and sprigs of holly for winter. Worked on 14-count Aida cloth, the finished design measures 14x16 inches. Instructions for the sampler begin on page 28 with the chart on pages 30–33.

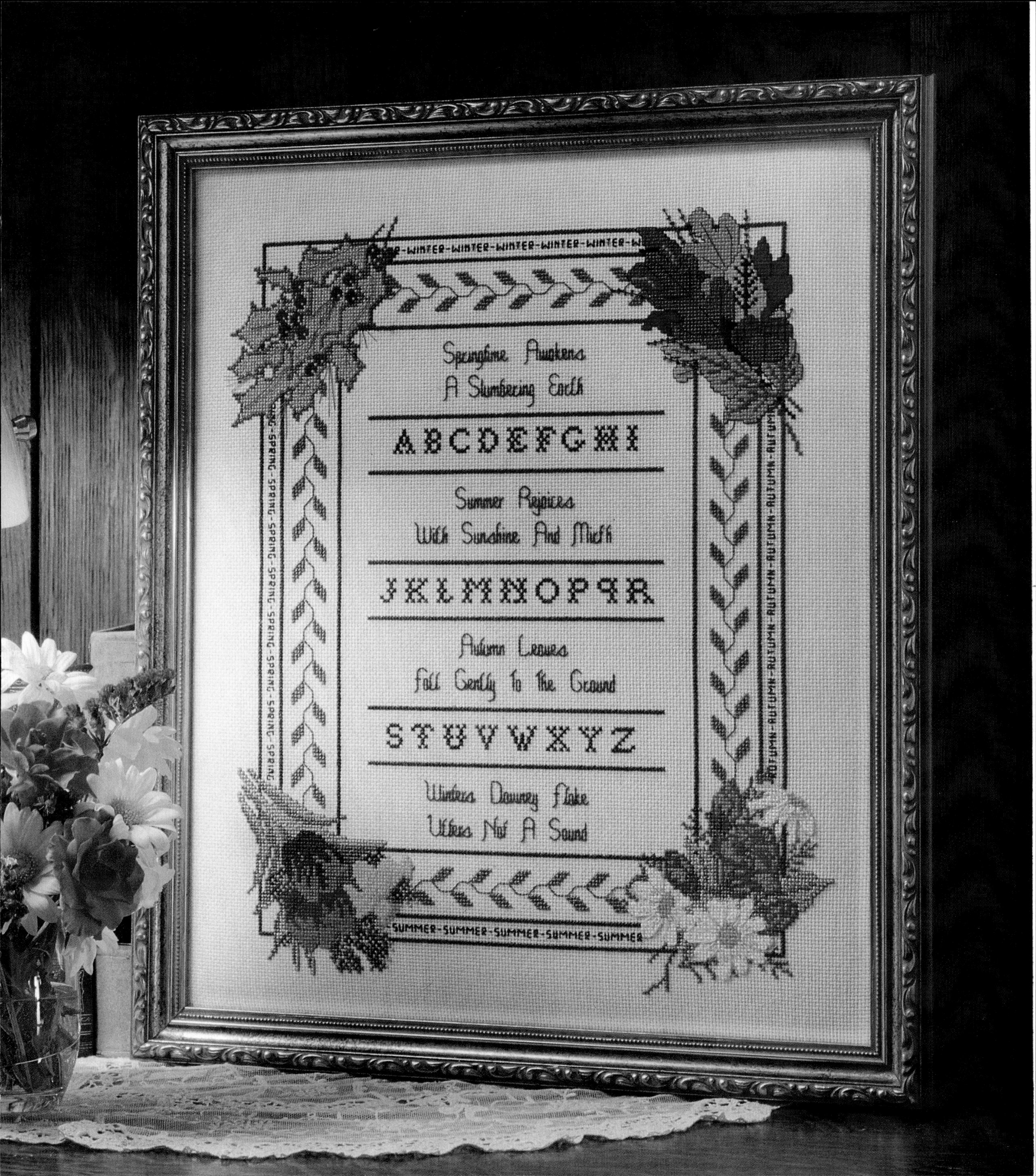

Springtime Awakens
A Slumbering Earth

ABCDEFGHI

Summer Rejoices
With Sunshine And Mirth

JKLMNOPQR

Autumn Leaves
Fall Gently to the Ground

STUVWXYZ

Winters Downy Flake
Utters Not A Sound

-WINTER-WINTER-WINTER-WINTER-WINTER-W

-SUMMER-SUMMER-SUMMER-SUMMER-SUMMER-

Mixed motifs of varying—and often illogical—proportions add to the charm of early samplers. No one knows whether the stitchers' intentions were to display skill or merely to fill odd spaces, but the results are captivating.

Mary Montgomery's 1906 sampler, *right,* provides the imagery—home and family—for the "things" that the Robert Louis Stevenson verse on the sampler immortalizes. Instructions begin on page 36.

The more contemporary wall hanging, *below,* features a floral border and an Old English alphabet. Worked on hardanger over two threads, the finished stitchery measures 12x16½ inches. Instructions for the floral sampler start on page 34.

A heart border frames the Sunshine Sampler, *opposite.* Personalize the 15x20-inch wall hanging with your own name and date of completion. Instructions for this project begin on page 26.

SUNSHINE SAMPLER

Shown on page 25.
Finished size of design area is 15x20 inches.
Design is 167x219 stitches.

MATERIALS

21x26 inches of hardanger fabric
DMC embroidery floss in colors listed
    on the color key; number of skeins
    required appears in parentheses
Tapestry needle
Embroidery hoop

INSTRUCTIONS

The chart for the sampler on page 25 is
divided into sections and printed on pages
26–29. Shaded areas on the charts show
you where the sections overlap. Do not
rework the shaded rows as you move from
section to section. These areas are only
placement guides.

Hem or tape raw edges of fabric to prevent threads from raveling as you work.
Use two strands of floss and work all
cross-stitches and backstitches over two
threads of fabric.

Measure 3 inches down and 3 inches in
from the top left corner of the cloth. Begin
stitching the upper left-hand corner of the
border here.

Backstitch the fence and the outlines of
the windows and door with No. 414 gray.

Backstitch the outline of the yard and
sidewalk in front of the house with No.
993 light green.

Backstitch "stitched by" and the year
with No. 991 green. Using your favorite
alphabet from this book or any other,
chart and stitch your name in green.

Backstitch the rays of the sun and the
birds' legs, beaks, and feet with No. 743
yellow. Backstitch the stems of the flowers
in the yard with No. 991 green.

Backstitch points on tulip petals with
No. 760 peach and No. 743 yellow to
match tulip cross-stitch color shown on
chart.

When stitching is complete, remove
tape. Press stitchery on wrong side, using
a damp cloth and warm iron. Frame as
desired.

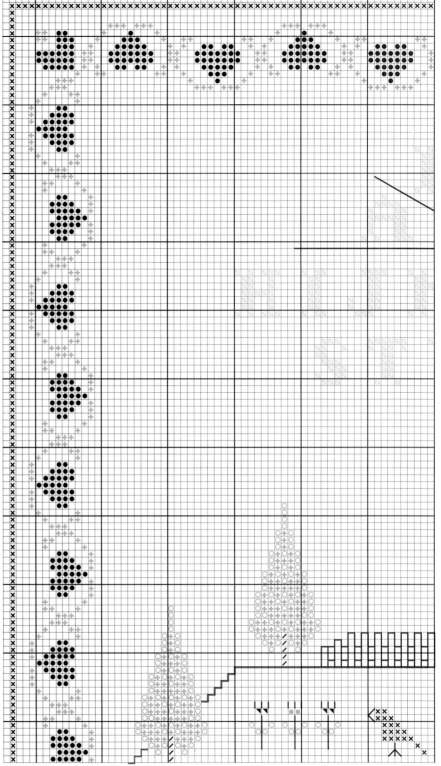

SUNSHINE SAMPLER

1 Square = 1 Stitch

COLOR KEY

▣	Peach 760 (1)	⊠	Blue 322 (1)	⧄	Brown 780 (1)
▶ White (1)	●	Red 347 (1)	◎	Green 991 (1)	⧄ Gray 414 (1)
◤ Yellow 743 (1)	▦	Purple 333 (1)	⊞	Light Green 993 (2)	

FOUR-SEASONS SAMPLER

Shown on pages 22 and 23.
Finished size of design area is 14x16 inches.
Design is 191x222 stitches.

MATERIALS

20x22 inches of 14-count ecru Aida cloth
DMC embroidery floss in colors listed on the color key; number of skeins required appears in parentheses
Tapestry needle
Embroidery hoop

INSTRUCTIONS

The chart for the sampler is divided into sections and printed on pages 30–33. Shaded areas show you where the sections overlap. Do not rework the shaded rows as you move from section to section. These areas are only placement guides.

Hem or tape raw edges of fabric to prevent threads from raveling. Use two strands of floss and work all cross-stitches over one thread of fabric. Work backstitches for lettering and for vine running through the leaves using two strands of floss. Use one strand for backstitches around leaves and flowers. Work long stitches and French knots with one strand. (See page 216 for stitch diagrams.)

Measure 3 inches down and 3½ inches in from the top left corner of the cloth. Begin stitching the upper left-hand corner of the border here. Arrows on pattern on page 30 show you where to begin.

BACKSTITCHES (Red lines on diagram): Backstitch names of the seasons around the border with No. 701 green.

Backstitch the center poem with No. 349 apple red. Outline the autumn leaves with No. 938 brown. Stitch around lavender tulip with No. 552 purple; coral tulip with No. 350 coral; and daffodil with No. 741 yellow-orange. Backstitch the trailing vine in the leaf border, the leaves in the tulip bouquet, and the leaves in the daisy bouquet with No. 701 green.

continued on page 34

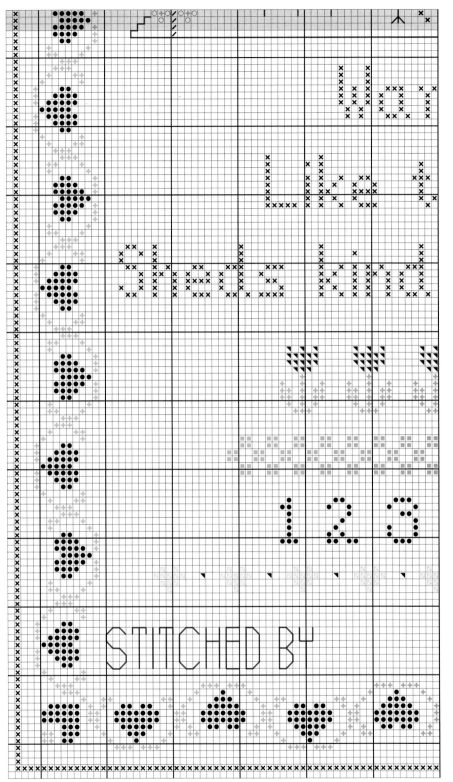

SUNSHINE SAMPLER

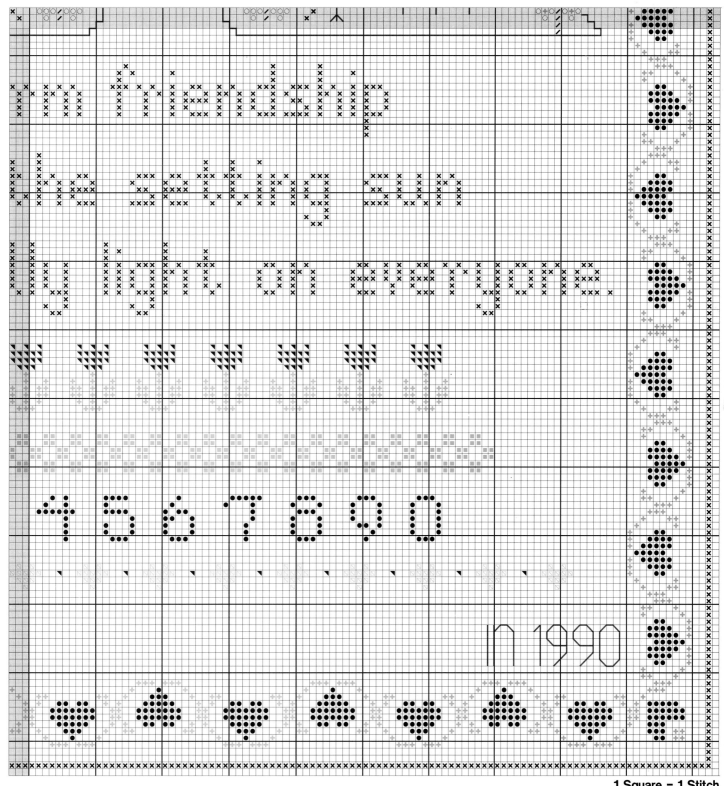

1 Square = 1 Stitch

COLOR KEY

▶ White (1)	☐ Peach 760 (1)	☒ Blue 322 (1)	☑ Brown 780 (1)
◤ Yellow 743 (1)	◉ Red 347 (1)	◎ Green 991 (1)	☐ Gray 414 (1)
	☐ Purple 333 (1)	⊞ Light Green 993 (2)	

29

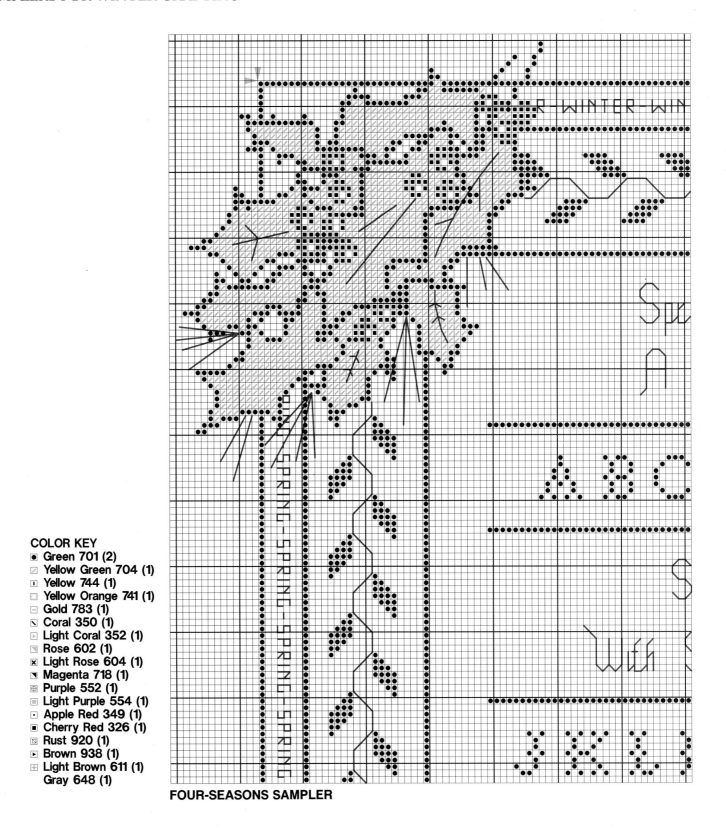

COLOR KEY
- ◉ Green 701 (2)
- ◪ Yellow Green 704 (1)
- ▯ Yellow 744 (1)
- ▢ Yellow Orange 741 (1)
- ⊟ Gold 783 (1)
- ◹ Coral 350 (1)
- ▷ Light Coral 352 (1)
- ◪ Rose 602 (1)
- ⊠ Light Rose 604 (1)
- ◣ Magenta 718 (1)
- ⊕ Purple 552 (1)
- ▦ Light Purple 554 (1)
- ⊡ Apple Red 349 (1)
- ◼ Cherry Red 326 (1)
- ◲ Rust 920 (1)
- ▶ Brown 938 (1)
- ⊞ Light Brown 611 (1)
- Gray 648 (1)

FOUR-SEASONS SAMPLER

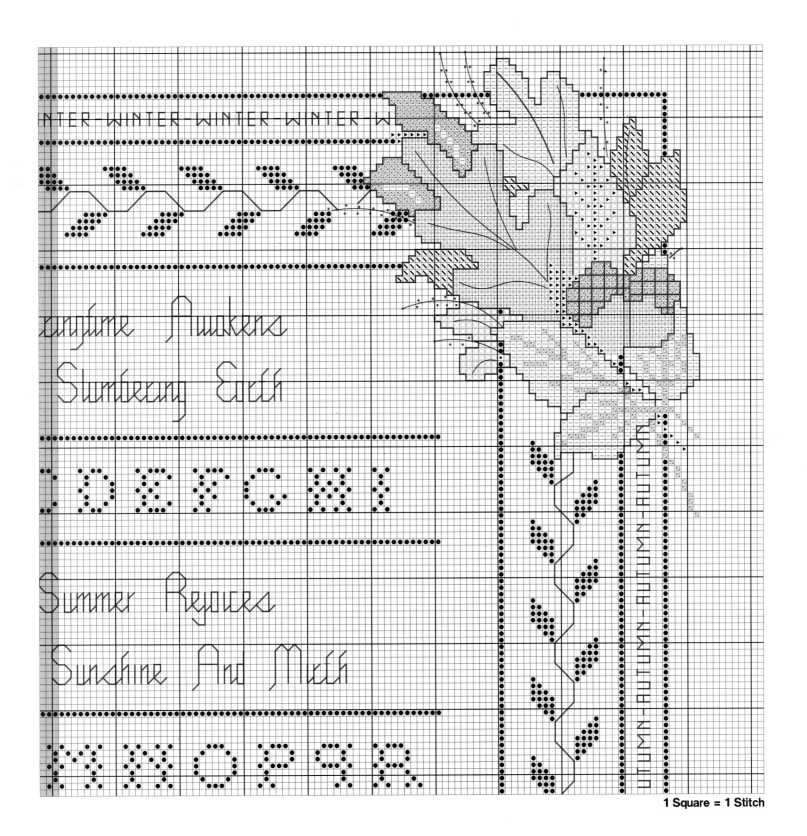

NTER·WINTER·WINTER·WINTER·W

eangtime Awakens

Slumbering Earth

D E F G H I

Summer Rejoices

Sunshine And Mirth

M N O P Q R

AUTUMN·AUTUMN·AUTUMN·AUTUM

1 Square = 1 Stitch

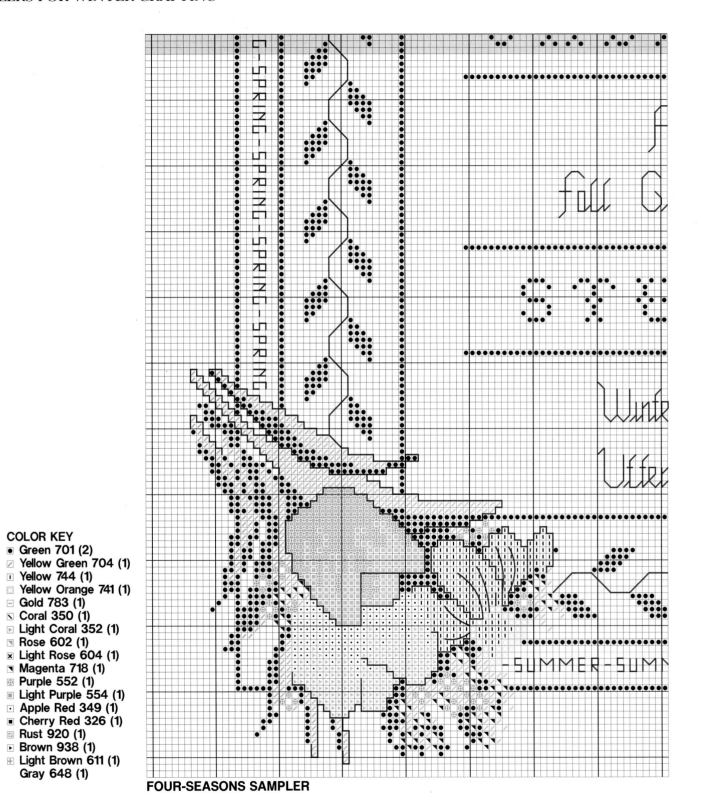

COLOR KEY
- ◉ Green 701 (2)
- ◨ Yellow Green 704 (1)
- ◦ Yellow 744 (1)
- ◨ Yellow Orange 741 (1)
- ⊟ Gold 783 (1)
- ◥ Coral 350 (1)
- ▷ Light Coral 352 (1)
- ◲ Rose 602 (1)
- ⊠ Light Rose 604 (1)
- ◣ Magenta 718 (1)
- ⊕ Purple 552 (1)
- ▦ Light Purple 554 (1)
- ◌ Apple Red 349 (1)
- ■ Cherry Red 326 (1)
- ◩ Rust 920 (1)
- ▸ Brown 938 (1)
- ⊞ Light Brown 611 (1)
- Gray 648 (1)

FOUR-SEASONS SAMPLER

Autumn Leaves
Gently To The Ground

Y Y W X Y Z

Falls Downy Flake
Was Not A Sound

AUTUMN-AUTUMN-AUTUMN-AU

MER-SUMMER-SUMMER-SUMMER

1 Square = 1 Stitch

continued from page 28
LONG STITCHES (long red lines on diagram): Stitch sprigs of holly with No. 701 green. Stitch veins in autumn leaves and stems of bittersweet with No. 938 brown. Long-stitch outline and veins of daisy petals in No. 648 gray. Stitch veins in daffodil petals with No. 741 yellow-orange.

FRENCH KNOTS: Make French knots along the bittersweet stems among the autumn leaves with No. 349 apple red.

FINISHING: When stitching is complete, remove tape from stitchery. Press stitchery on wrong side, using a damp cloth and warm iron. Frame as desired.

FLORAL BORDER SAMPLER

Shown on page 24.
Finished size of design area is 12x16½ inches.
Design is 130x182 stitches.

MATERIALS
18x23 inches of hardanger fabric
DMC embroidery floss in colors listed on the color key; number of skeins required appears in parentheses
Tapestry needle
Embroidery hoop

INSTRUCTIONS
The pattern for the sampler on page 24 is located at *right*. Shaded rows on the chart, *opposite*, show you where the two sections overlap. Do not rework the shaded rows as you move from section to section. This area is only a placement guide.

Hem or tape raw edges of fabric to prevent threads from raveling as you work. Use three strands of floss and work all cross-stitches over two threads of fabric.

Measure 3 inches down and 3 inches in from the top left corner of the cloth. Begin stitching the upper left-hand flower here. The arrow shows you where to begin.

When stitching is complete, remove tape. Press on wrong side, using a damp cloth and warm iron. Frame as desired.

COLOR KEY

▲ Rose 601 (1)
Ⅰ Light Rose 604 (2)
▢ Mahogany 221 (1)

◪ Light Mahogany 224 (1)
⊞ Green 991 (2)
⊕ Navy 311 (1)
☒ Periwinkle 792 (1)

⊟ Light Periwinkle 794 (1)
▨ Brown 780 (1)
■ Gold 676 (1)

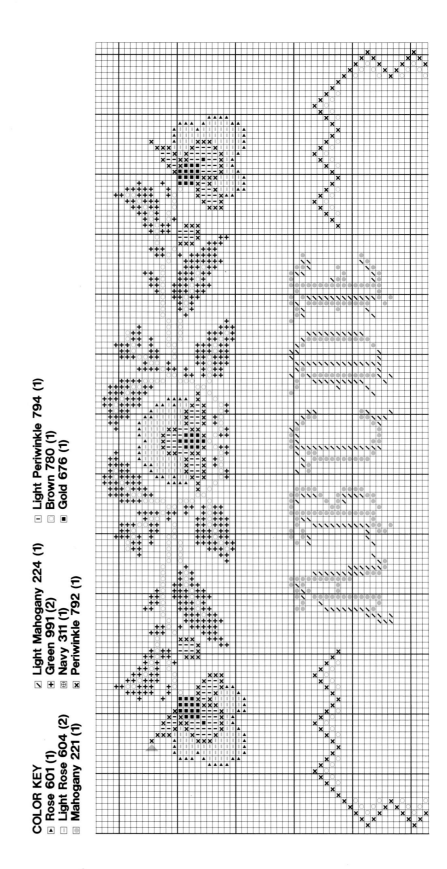

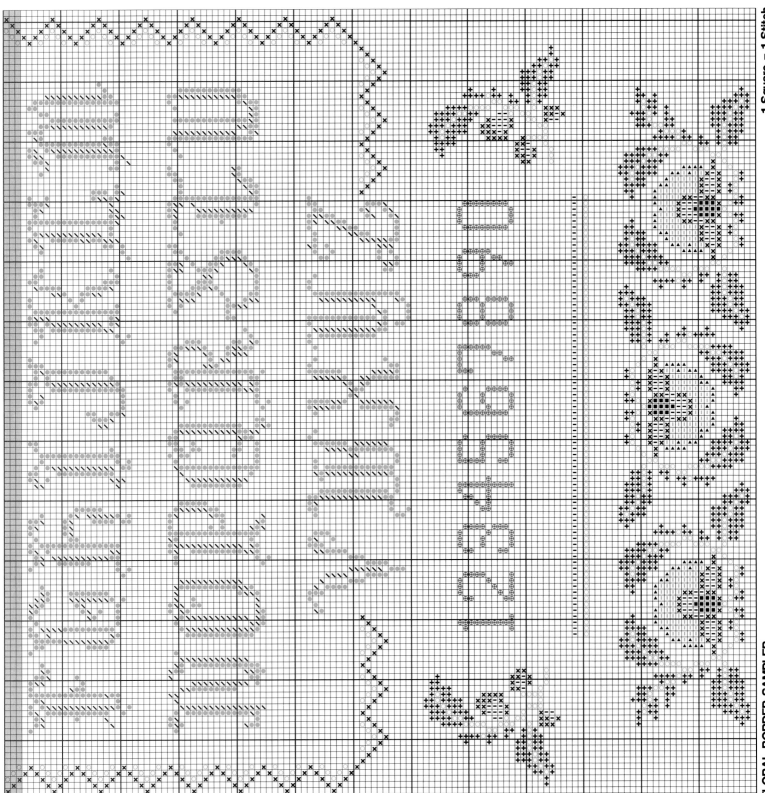

FLORAL BORDER SAMPLER

MARY MONTGOMERY SAMPLER

Shown on page 24.
Finished size of design is 8½x12 inches.
Design is 118x166 stitches.

MATERIALS

15x18 inches of ecru 14-count Aida
    cloth
DMC embroidery floss in colors listed
    on the color key; number of skeins
    required appears in parentheses
Tapestry needle
Embroidery hoop

INSTRUCTIONS

The chart for the sampler is divided into
two sections *at right.*

The shaded rows on the chart, *opposite,*
show you where the sections overlap. Do
not rework the shaded rows as you move
from section to section. This area is only a
placement guide.

Hem or tape raw edges of fabric to prevent threads from raveling as you work.
Use two strands of floss and work all
cross-stitches and backstitches over one
thread of fabric.

Measure 3 inches down and 3 inches in
from the top left corner of the cloth. Begin
stitching the upper left-hand corner of the
border here.

Reproduce the antique sampler as it is
with Mary Montgomery's name and year
of completion, or use the alphabets and
numbers on the sampler to personalize
your work with your own name and the
current year.

BACKSTITCHES (red lines on chart):
(See stitch diagram on page 216.) Backstitch the faces and hands of the people
and the bird's head and tail with No. 433
dark brown.

When stitching is complete, remove
tape. Press stitchery on wrong side, using
a damp cloth and warm iron. Frame as
desired.

COLOR KEY
▲ Gold 972 (1)
▣ Dark Brown 433 (2)
■ Brown 436 (1)
▨ Blue 930 (1)
✚ Green 580 (1)

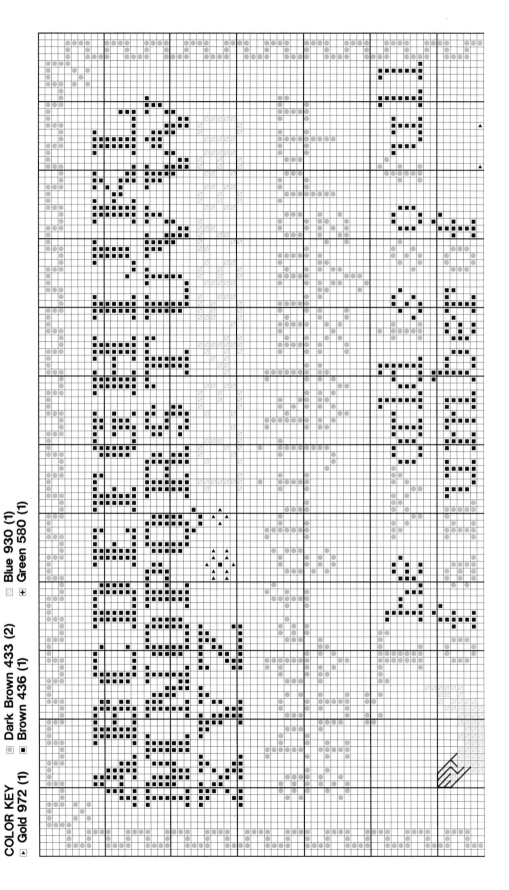

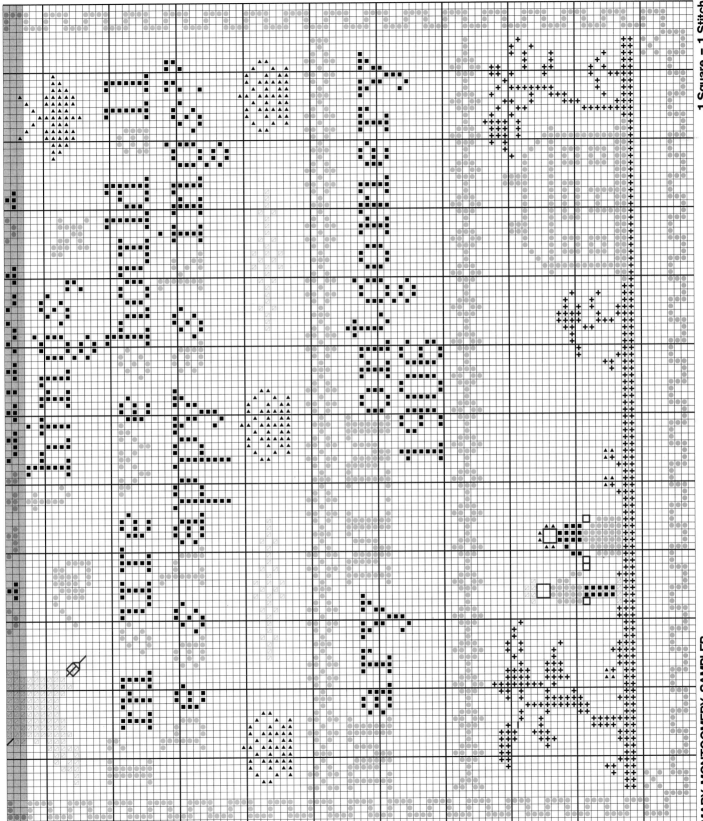

1 Square = 1 Stitch

MARY MONTGOMERY SAMPLER

37

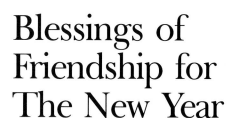

Blessings of Friendship for The New Year

You probably count your friends among your greatest blessings. Why not share your feelings in cross-stitch?

The mini-samplers, *above,* are quick and easy to make and carry messages perfect for gift giving.

Filled with photos of friends and family, the album, *opposite,* invites visitors to share in happy memories. Designed to fit a 7x9¼-inch photo album, the cross-stitched cover is heavily embellished with a colorful garden of lazy daisy and French knot flowers.

Patterns for these projects begin on page 48.

Tender Sentiments for Valentine's Day

Choose from romantic hearts-and-flowers designs in our collection to express loving thoughts to your sweetheart.

A delicate piece of embroidery from the Victorian era inspired the designs, *opposite.* A ruffled heart-shaped pillow features a rose garland worked in cross-stitches on 14-count Aida cloth.

By repeating the design twice and changing the colors ever so slightly, you can create the half-cross-stitched photo mat on perforated paper.

Tuck an old-fashioned foldout valentine card like these, *above,* into your handmade gift for an added sentimental touch.

Instructions begin on page 54.

Tender Sentiments for Valentine's Day

Express your love this Valentine's Day with gifts of everlasting, hand-stitched roses.

An antique filet-crocheted doily provided the pattern for the circle of roses, *above.* Measuring only 13 inches in diameter, the design is worked on 18-count Aida cloth, each stitch embroidered over two threads of fabric. Flowers are worked in variegated pink thread to give added dimension.

The heart-shaped wreath of roses, *opposite,* measures a full 19x20 inches, framed as shown. Shades of cranberry and sea-foam green stand out against a white hardanger background.

Instructions begin on page 54.

42

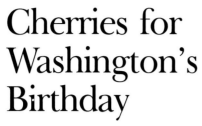

Cherries for Washington's Birthday

The familiar story of George Washington and the cherry tree teaches us the importance of always telling the truth.

Even small children are taught the merits of honesty. How many times were we told about George's noble decision to admit he had cut down the cherry tree with his own small hatchet?

The sampler, *above,* is a gentle reminder as well as a handsome decorating accessory. Worked on 18-count Floba cloth, the finished design measures 14¾x5 inches.

The cherry and leaf motif from the sampler embellishes a purchased dresser jar,

right. The jar has a 3½-inch insert designed for needlework and is available in crafts shops. Instructions begin on page 56 with a pattern on pages 58 and 59.

Everyone knows there are only so many accidents you can blame on the family pet. The saying on the framed cross-stitch piece, *above,* gives the cat credit (or blame) for just about everything that happens. Stitched on 14-count Aida cloth, the framed piece measures 15¾x8¾ inches. Instructions for this project are on page 61 with a pattern on page 63.

St. Patrick's Day Good-Luck Wishes

The luck of the Irish will be with the lad or lassie who receives one of these shamrock-design gifts. Good health and happiness are perfect wishes for every season of the year.

The men in your family will enjoy the walnut box, *right,* for jewelry, stationery, pens, and all the other treasures they tuck away. The 7x5-inch box comes with a lid insert designed for needlework. The sampler, *opposite,* carries the same central motif, surrounded by a shamrock border. Worked on 14-count Aida cloth, the sampler, framed as shown, measures 15x18½ inches.

Patterns and instructions for these projects begin on page 58.

FRIENDSHIP SAMPLER

COLOR KEY
- ⊞ Green 500
- ▣ Peach 402
- ◉ Rust 919
- ⊠ Cream 746
- ■ Burgundy 814
- ▢ Teal 502

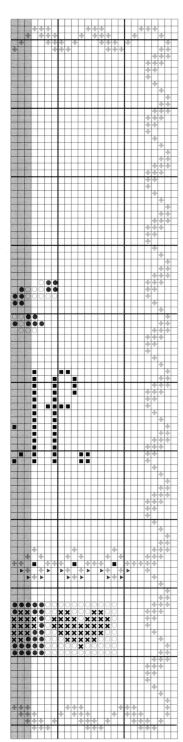

1 Square = 1 Stitch

FRIENDSHIP SAMPLER

Shown on page 38.
Finished size of stitched area is 7x5½ inches.
Design is 127x103 stitches.

MATERIALS
13x12-inch piece of tan 18-count even-weave fabric (Aida)
One skein of DMC embroidery floss in colors listed on the color key
Tapestry needle
Embroidery hoop

INSTRUCTIONS
Hem or tape raw edges of fabric to prevent raveling.

Refer to the chart, *left,* for stitching the sampler. The chart is in two sections. Shaded stitches on page 49 are only a guide to help you move from one part of the chart to the other. Do not rework these rows of stitches.

Measure down 3 inches and in 3 inches from the upper left corner of the fabric. Begin stitching the upper left corner of the design here.

Use two strands of floss to work the cross-stitches over one thread of fabric.

Press finished stitchery on the back side. Frame as desired.

HEARTS SAMPLER

Shown on page 38.
Finished size of stitched area is 7½x5½ inches.
Design is 138x98 stitches.

MATERIALS
12x14-inch piece of pale blue-gray 18-count even-weave fabric
One skein of DMC embroidery floss in colors listed on the color key
Tapestry needle
Embroidery hoop

INSTRUCTIONS
Tape raw edges of fabric to prevent raveling. The chart for the sampler is on pages 50 and 51 and is divided into two parts. Shaded rows of stitches on page 51 are repeated from page 50 and are used to guide you in moving from one section to the next. Do not restitch these shaded rows.

Measure down 3 inches and in 3 inches from the upper left corner of the fabric. Begin stitching the upper left corner of the design here.

Using two strands of floss, work stitches over one thread of fabric.

Press finished stitchery on the back side. Frame as desired.

HEARTS SAMPLER

COLOR KEY
- ▪ Teal 924
- ◉ Rust 221
- ⊞ Medium Pink 223
- ⊠ Light Pink 225

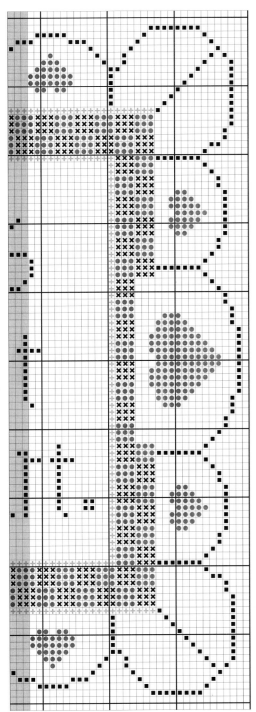

1 Square = 1 Stitch

"WELCOME, GUEST" BOOK COVER

Shown on page 39.
Finished book measures 7x9¼ inches.
Design is 79x103 stitches.

MATERIALS

13x16-inch rectangle of white hardanger
DMC embroidery floss in colors listed
   on the color key; number of skeins
   required appears in parentheses
Embroidery hoop
Tapestry needle
Purchased scrapbook or photograph
   album
White hardanger, white cotton fabric,
   fleece, and narrow white piping to fit
   the photo album or scrapbook (see
   instructions, *right,* to determine
   amounts needed)

INSTRUCTIONS

Hem or tape the raw edges of the hardanger to prevent threads from raveling as you work.

The chart for the design appears on page 52. Measure 3 inches down and 3 inches in from the upper left corner of the fabric; begin stitching upper left border here.

Use two strands of floss and work cross-stitches over two threads of fabric.

TO WORK DECORATIVE STITCHES: French knots appear as red dots on the pattern; lazy daisy stitches appear as loops. Use four strands of embroidery floss to work French knots and two strands of embroidery floss to work backstitches and lazy daisy stitches. *Note:* Stitch diagrams appear on page 216.

With No. 3021 brown, work French knot flower centers.

Note: To keep the French knots on the top side of the sampler, pull the thread up through a hole in the fabric, wrap the thread around the needle, and reinsert the needle into either the hole or the thread just above the hole.

With brown floss, backstitch the garden path.

Using the photograph as a guide for color selections, work lazy daisy stitches for flower petals and French knots for clusters of flower buds. Randomly select colors of embroidery floss for flowers.

With No. 368 green floss, work lazy daisy stitches for leaves; work backstitches for the stems.

When stitching is complete, press the piece on the back side using a warm iron and a damp cloth.

TO FINISH BOOK COVER: Draw three rectangles onto brown paper as follows: Draw one the size of the album front cover, another the size of the spine, and the third the length of the front cover and five inches wide (inner flap). Add ½-inch seam allowances to patterns; cut out.

From the unstitched hardanger, cut one large rectangle for the back cover; cut the embroidered sampler the same size. Cut one spine and two flaps from the unstitched hardanger. Cut matching shapes from fleece.

Baste fleece pieces to wrong sides of corresponding hardanger pieces.

Sew piping to *each* long edge of the spine piece. With right sides together, sew album front and back pieces to spine. Trim seams to ¼ inch.

From white cotton fabric, cut lining to match the assembled cover.

On one long side of *each* inner flap piece, press under ¼ inch twice; machine-hem. With right sides together and raw edges even, sew piping around assembled cover. With right sides facing, sew flaps to ends of cover.

Pin right side of lining atop wrong sides of flaps. Sew lining (through all thicknesses) atop the piping seam, leaving an opening for turning. Clip the corners, turn the piece to the right side, and press; slip-stitch the opening closed. Slip flaps over album cover.

"WELCOME, GUEST" BOOK COVER

1 Square = 1 Stitch

COLOR KEY

- ⊠ Dark Green 319 (1)
- ▨ Medium Green 367 (1)
- ⊟ Olive Green 470 (1)
- ⊡ Green 368 (1)
- ▣ Dark Coral 349 (1)
- ● Brown 3021 (2)

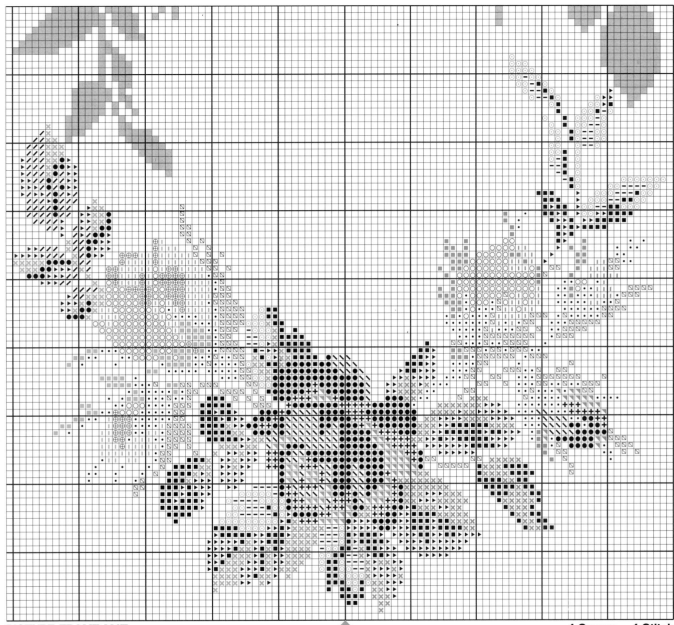

PICTURE FRAME MAT

1 Square = 1 Stitch

COLOR KEY (Frame)
- ⊠ Dark Blue Green 500
- ◉ Blue Green 502
- ▷ Sea Foam 368
- ◪ Light Sea Foam 369
- ▣ Forest Green 986
- ▪ Moss Green 580
- ▢ Olive Green 733
- ▬ Green Gold 833
- ▨ Light Gold 3046

- ⊡ Light Brown 420
- ▨ Brown 610
- ◹ Dark Garnet 814
- ✛ Garnet 816
- ◖ Dark Coral 817
- ◺ Coral 350
- ⊟ Yellow Gold 742
- ⊕ Gold 783
- ◎ Yellow 725

COLOR KEY (Pillow)
- ⊠ Dark Blue Green 500
- ◉ Blue Green 502
- ▷ Sea Foam 368
- ◪ Light Sea Foam 369
- ▣ Forest Green 986
- ▪ Moss Green 580
- ▢ Olive Green 733
- ▬ Green Gold 833
- ▨ Light Gold 3046

- ⊡ Light Brown 420
- ▨ Brown 610
- ◹ Copper 921
- ✛ Light Copper 402
- ◖ Yellow 743
- ◺ Light Yellow 745
- ⊟ Dark Plum 915
- ⊕ Mauve 316
- ◎ Light Mauve 778

VICTORIAN ROSES HEART PILLOW

Shown on page 41.
Finished size, including ruffle, is approximately 15x18 inches.
Design is 99x82 stitches.

MATERIALS
19-inch square of brown 14-count Aida cloth
One skein of DMC embroidery floss in colors listed on the color key
Embroidery hoop; tapestry needle
Note: Yardages are for 45-inch-wide fabrics:
1 yard of paisley fabric (backing, ruffle)
¾ yard of green taffeta (ruffle)
½ yard of fleece
1 yard of narrow purple piping
Polyester fiberfill
Water-erasable marking pen
Graph paper

INSTRUCTIONS
Note: One flower garland on the chart on page 53 is used for the heart pillow. (See the photograph on page 41.)

On graph paper, draw a heart pattern that measures 13 inches at its widest point and 10 inches tall from the inverted point to the tip of the heart.

Hem or tape raw edges of Aida cloth to prevent threads from raveling.

Cut out heart pattern. Trace heart outline, centered, onto Aida cloth using the water-erasable pen.

Measure 3 inches up from bottom tip of heart; begin working cross-stitches here, starting with the square marked with an arrow on pattern on page 53.

Use two strands of floss and work cross-stitches over one thread of fabric.

When embroidery is complete, baste fleece lining to wrong side of stitchery on outline (seam line). Cut out heart ½ inch beyond seam line for seam allowance.

Cut matching back from paisley print fabric. Set aside.

Sew piping to seam line on heart front. Cut 6-inch-wide bias paisley strips and 5-inch-wide bias taffeta strips that measure twice the perimeter of heart for ruffles. Piece and sew each ruffle fabric into circle.

Press each ruffle in half lengthwise, wrong sides together. Place small taffeta ruffle atop large paisley ruffle.

Divide and mark ruffle into two equal parts; sew two rows of gathering threads ¼ and ½ inch from raw edges on each part. Gather the ruffle and stitch to seam line atop piping. With masking tape, tape ruffle flat to front side of heart.

Sew pillow back to front, leaving an opening for turning. Trim seams, clip curves; turn pillow to right side. Remove masking tape; press. Stuff firmly with polyester fiberfill and slip-stitch opening closed.

VICTORIAN ROSES PICTURE FRAME MAT

Shown on page 41.
Finished size, unframed, is 9x12 inches.
Design is 99x146 stitches.

MATERIALS
One sheet of 9x12-inch brown perforated paper
One skein of DMC embroidery floss in colors listed on the color key
Tapestry needle

INSTRUCTIONS
Note: The top and bottom of the mat are 9 inches wide. Sides are 12 inches long. When piece is finished there will be approximately 11 rows remaining beyond last row of stitching along top and bottom and 15 rows remaining on each side.

Refer to chart on page 53 for stitching. Locate center of bottom edge of perforated paper and count up 11 rows; begin stitching here. The arrow indicates where to begin on the chart. Using three strands of floss, work half-cross stitches over one square of paper. Refer to stitch diagram on page 216.

Stitch bottom portion of mat from pattern on page 53. Then turn pattern upside down and work top half. The shaded portions of the leaves at the top of the design are stitched following the symbols indicated. Use the shading for placement only when stitching the top half.

When stitching is complete, mount photograph and frame as desired.

ROSE DOILY

Shown on page 42.
Finished diameter of doily is 13 inches.
Design is 90x90 stitches.

MATERIALS
16-inch square of white 18-count Aida cloth
16-inch square of white cotton batiste fabric (backing)
16-inch square of lightweight woven interfacing
DMC embroidery floss in colors listed on the color key; number of skeins required appears in parentheses
Embroidery hoop; tapestry needle
1½ yards of ⅝-inch-wide white lace
1½ yards of ⅛-inch-wide pink satin ribbon
Water-erasable marking pen

INSTRUCTIONS
Hem or tape raw edges of Aida cloth to prevent threads from raveling.

The chart for the design is on page 55. Use four strands of floss and work cross-stitches over two threads of fabric.

Locate center of chart and center of fabric; begin stitching here. (See arrows on chart.) When stitching is complete, draw a 12-inch-diameter circle pattern on paper; cut out. Center and trace circle onto stitched piece using the water-erasable pen. Add ½ inch beyond marking for seam allowances and cut out. With right sides facing, sew lace atop seam line.

Trace circle (for seam line) onto interfacing; sew interfacing to wrong side of backing fabric on seam line. Cut out ½ inch from seam.

With right sides facing, sew stitchery to backing, leaving an opening for turning. Trim seam to ¼ inch; clip seams, and turn to right side. Press; sew opening closed.

Tie satin ribbon into six small bows; sew to points of design.

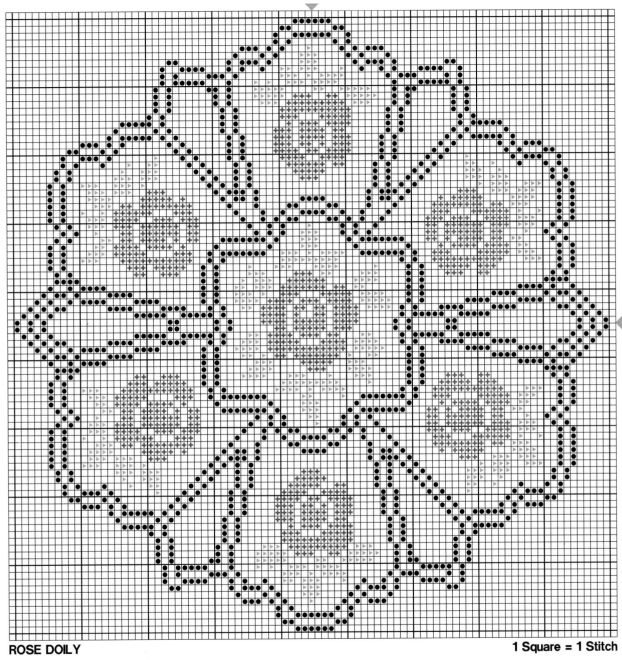

ROSE DOILY

1 Square = 1 Stitch

COLOR KEY
- ⊡ Dark Green 562 (1)
- ◉ Medium Green 563 (2)
- ⊞ Pink 99 (2)

ROSE HEART WREATH

Shown on page 43.
Finished size, framed, is 19x20 inches.
Design is 138x151 stitches.

MATERIALS

25x26-inch piece of white 22-count
  even-weave fabric (hardanger)
DMC embroidery floss in colors listed
  on the color key; number of skeins
  required appears in parentheses
Embroidery hoop
Tapestry needle

INSTRUCTIONS

Pattern for wreath is on pages 56–59. It is divided into four sections. Shaded stitches will help you move from chart to chart. Do not rework the shaded stitches.

Hem or tape raw edges of fabric to prevent threads from raveling as you work. Use two strands of floss and work cross-stitches over two threads of fabric.

Locate the center of the fabric and the center of the design; begin stitching here. Arrows on the charts mark the center. Stitch "I Love You" first, then count out to the wreath of roses.

When stitching is complete, remove tape. Carefully press stitchery on wrong side. Frame as desired.

HONESTY SAMPLER

Shown on page 44.
Finished size of design is 14¾x5 inches.
Design is 45x134 stitches.

MATERIALS

11x22 inches of 18-count Aida cloth
  (fabric shown is Zweigart's Floba)
One skein of DMC embroidery floss in
  colors listed on the color key
Tapestry needle
Embroidery hoop

INSTRUCTIONS

The chart for the Honesty Sampler is located on pages 58 and 59. It is divided into two sections. Three rows of stitches are shaded on the pattern on page 59. The shaded stitches are to guide you in matching the two pattern pieces. Do not rework these stitches as you move from one section to the other.

Hem or tape raw edges of fabric to prevent threads from raveling as you work.

Measure 3 inches down and 3 inches in from the top left corner of the fabric. Begin stitching the upper left corner of the border here.

Work all cross-stitches using three strands of embroidery floss over two threads of fabric. Backstitch motto using three strands of black floss. Backstitch cherry stems and veins in leaves using two strands of black floss.

Press stitchery; frame as desired.

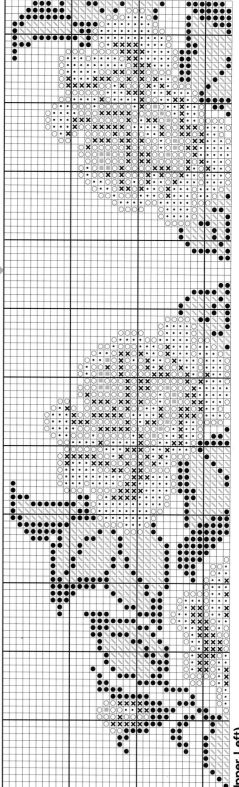

COLOR KEY
◻ Dark Cranberry 600 (2)
☒ Cranberry 602 (2)
⊡ Mauve 3689 (1)
▣ Coral 325 (2)
○ Dark Seafoam 561 (2)
● Seafoam 563 (2)

(Upper Left)

ROSE HEART WREATH (Lower Left)

CHERRIES DRESSER JAR INSERT

Shown on page 45.
Finished size of design is 2¼x3 inches.
Design is 25x34 stitches.

MATERIALS

Wooden or ceramic jar with lid designed for needlework (available through needlework shops)
6x8-inch piece of ecru hardanger
One skein of DMC embroidery floss in colors listed on the color key (dark teal and gold are not used)
Tapestry needle
Embroidery hoop

INSTRUCTIONS

Note: The dresser jar shown on page 45 is from Anne Brinkley Designs, 21 Ransom Road, Newton Centre, MA 02159.

The cherry and leaf design is part of the Honesty Sampler pattern, *bottom right.*

Hem or tape raw edges of fabric to prevent threads from raveling as you work.

Use the arrows on the chart to locate the center of the design; locate the center of the fabric. Begin working here.

Use three strands of floss and work cross-stitches over two threads of fabric. Backstitch cherry stems and veins in leaves using two strands of No. 310 black.

Press the finished stitchery on the back side. Mount the stitchery in the jar top following the manufacturer's instructions.

SHAMROCK SAMPLER

Shown on page 47.
Finished design is 11¼x14¾ inches.
Design is 157x205 stitches.

MATERIALS

18x21-inch piece of ecru 14-count Aida cloth
DMC embroidery floss in colors listed on the color key; number of skeins required appears in parentheses
Tapestry needle; embroidery hoop

INSTRUCTIONS

The chart for the sampler is located on pages 60–63. It is divided into four sections. Work the top left portion on page 60 first. *Note:* Shaded areas on the second, third, and fourth sections are to guide you in moving from one section to the next. Do not rework these shaded areas.

Hem or tape raw edges of fabric to prevent threads from raveling as you work. Measure 3 inches down and 3 inches in from the top left corner of the cloth. Begin stitching the shamrock in the upper left-hand corner here.

Use two strands of floss and work cross-stitches and backstitches over one thread of fabric.

Backstitch the large "F," alphabet, numbers, and white flowers using two strands of No. 909 dark green floss. Backstitch the "Good Luck" message and the line between the alphabet and numbers using two strands of No. 553 violet.

Remove tape; press stitchery on wrong side. Frame as desired.

SHAMROCK BOX

Shown on page 46.
Finished size of design is 6¾x4¾ inches.
Design is 73x53 stitches.

MATERIALS

Box with lid designed for needlework (available at crafts shops)
11x10 inches of ecru hardanger
One skein of DMC embroidery floss in colors listed on the color key (No. 553 violet and No. 601 mauve are not needed for this project)
Tapestry needle
Embroidery hoop

continued

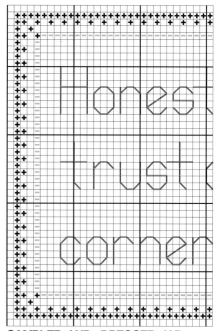

(Upper Right)

SAMPLER AND DRESSER JAR

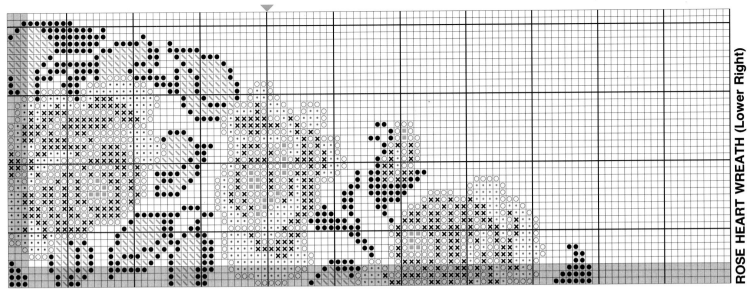

COLOR KEY

⊞	Dark Teal 561
⊟	Gold 676
◉	Green 905

◈	Light Green 907
⊠	Brown 400
▯	Red 498
◺	Coral 891

⊠	Pink 3326
	Black 310

COLOR KEY
◌	Dark Cranberry 600 (2)
✕	Cranberry 602 (2)
☐	Mauve 3689 (1)
◼	Coral 325 (2)
●	Dark Seafoam 561 (2)
◿	Seafoam 563 (2)

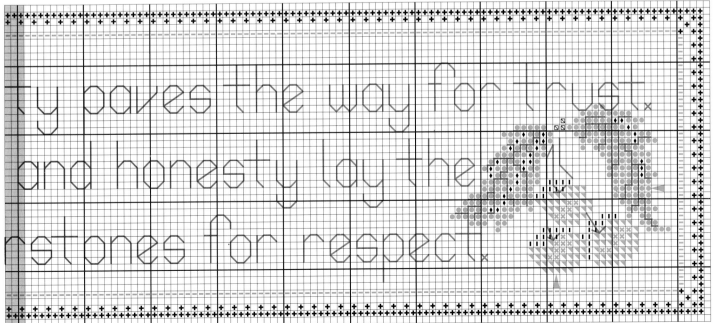

1 Square = 1 Stitch

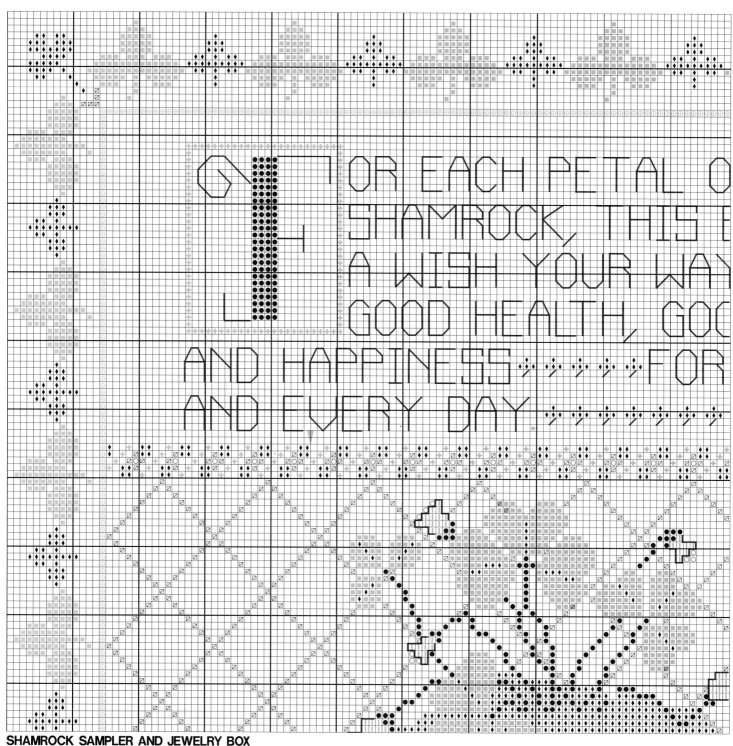

SHAMROCK SAMPLER AND JEWELRY BOX

COLOR KEY	Mauve 601 (1)	Lavender 340 (1)	Light Green 913 (2)
White (1)	Pink 3708 (1)	Dark Green 909 (2)	
Yellow 726 (1)	Violet 553 (1)	Medium Green 911 (2)	

1 Square = 1 Stitch

INSTRUCTIONS

Note: The jewelry box shown on page 46 is from Sudberry House, Old Lyme, Conn.

The pattern for the insert is the large shamrock motif from the Sampler pattern on pages 60–63. Arrows on the pattern mark the area to stitch for the box.

Hem or tape raw edges of fabric to prevent threads from raveling as you work.

Measure down 3 inches and in 3 inches from the upper left corner of the fabric. Begin stitching the top pink and green border here. Use three strands of floss and cross-stitch over two threads of fabric. Backstitch white flowers using two strands of No. 909 dark green.

Carefully press the finished stitchery on the back side. Mount in the box following the manufacturer's instructions.

"THE CAT DID IT" WALL HANGING

Shown on page 45.
Finished size of design is 12¾x6½ inches.
Design is 46x89 stitches.

MATERIALS

13x18-inch piece of ecru 14-count Aida cloth
One skein of DMC embroidery floss in colors listed on the color key
Tapestry needle
Embroidery hoop

INSTRUCTIONS

The chart for the project is located on page 63.

Hem or tape raw edges of fabric to prevent threads from raveling as you work.

Measure 3 inches down and 3 inches in from the top left corner of the fabric. Begin stitching the upper left-hand corner of the border here.

Use three strands of floss and work the cross-stitches over two threads of fabric. Backstitch cherry stems using two strands of No. 703 green and comma with two strands of No. 3371 black-brown.

Press finished stitchery on back side. Frame as desired.

SHAMROCK SAMPLER AND JEWELRY BOX

COLOR KEY

⊞ Mauve 601 (1)	☑ Lavender 340 (1)	⊡ Light Green 913 (2)	
⊡ White (1)	⊞ Pink 3708 (1)	● Dark Green 909 (2)	
◎ Yellow 726 (1)	⊛ Violet 553 (1)	▦ Medium Green 911 (2)	

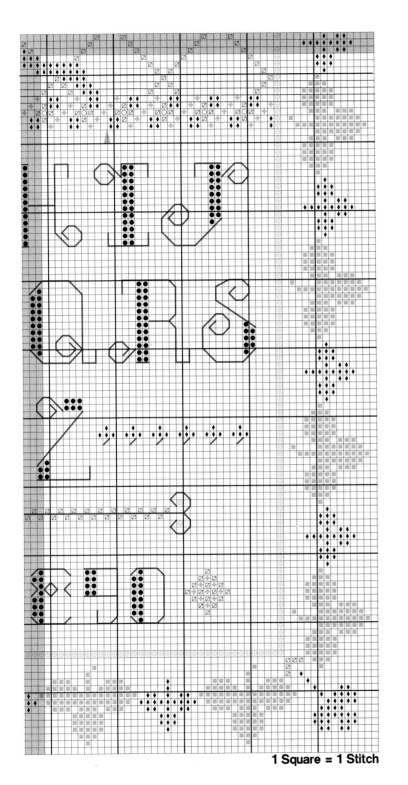

1 Square = 1 Stitch

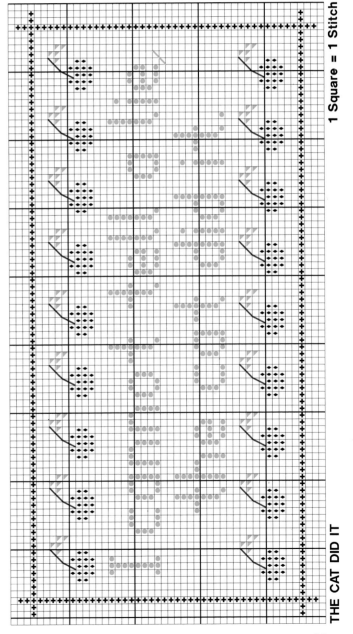

1 Square = 1 Stitch

THE CAT DID IT

63

Nature's Finest Gifts

SPRINGTIME'S BLESSINGS

Mother Nature does her finest work in the springtime. The earth awakens with color and growth when small purple crocuses peek through the soil and daffodils shoot above the new grass.

A stitched wreath of birds and flowers makes an elegant insert for the tabletop, *left.* Worked on a background of 30-count linen, the pastel array of embroidery floss mimics spring's refreshing colors. Instructions are on page 72 and include the source for ordering the table.

In the waning days of winter, chirping robins and budding flowers are true harbingers of spring's forthcoming arrival. Birds and posies offer cross-stitchers many colorful natural designs to adapt to fabric.

The small hearth stool, *left,* uses peach-colored 14-count Aida cloth for the background in a 6½x5½-inch design. Darker shades of floss outline the morning glories, leaves, and birds for emphasis.

Hanging above a table in the entry of your home, the mother robin in the mirror insert, *opposite,* will bid welcome to visitors. The mirror is a full 13¼x26 inches and holds a 12x9-inch piece of needlework. Patterns and instructions begin on page 74.

Nothing compares to the beauty of spring's first flowers. Their symmetry and bright colors–reds, greens, lavenders, and yellows–always inspire stitchers.

Traditionally, bell-pulls are done in crewelwork to show the details of flowers and herbs. The cross-stitched one, *opposite,* does the same, highlighting iris and tulips. The 7x30-inch length of 28-count linen provides a wonderful background for the shading of the flowers. Make cording to match with coordinating floss or pearl cotton.

The top of the jewelry box, *above,* is designed to hold a 10x7-inch piece of needlework. The floral oval with a monogrammed center makes this beautiful box a very personal gift.

Instructions for these projects begin on page 80.

If there's a universal floral symbol of springtime, it's likely the popular and venerable tulip. Alone, or in bunches, this stately flower shows strength and beauty.

Add pizzazz to a place mat, *below,* with a napkin and flatware pocket featuring the tulip motif. Cross-stitch the tulips on 14-count Aida cloth. Then, use it to make a pocket for your silverware on a handmade or purchased place mat.

Show your attention to detail by stitching a matching border for curtain panels, *opposite.* Worked on 14-count Aida cloth, each finished square of tulips measures 3⅞x3⅞ inches.

Instructions begin on page 77.

CIRCLE OF BIRDS TABLE INSERT

Shown on pages 64 and 65.
Finished size of stitchery is approximately 9½ inches square.
Design is 142x148 stitches.

MATERIALS

15½-inch square of ecru even-weave linen with 30 threads per inch
One skein of DMC embroidery floss in colors listed on the color key
Table with 11½-inch-square insert for needlework (available through crafts shops or write to Plain n' Fancy, P.O. Box 357, Mathews, VA 23109)
Embroidery hoop; tapestry needle

INSTRUCTIONS

The complete chart for the Circle of Birds appears at *right* and is divided into two sections. Work all of the section on page 72 first, then finish with page 73. Three shaded rows of stitches on page 73 represent the overlap of the two sections. Do not repeat these stitches when working the design.

Measure 4 inches down and 4½ inches in from the upper left corner of the fabric. Begin stitching here. Arrows on the pattern show you where to start.

Use two strands of floss and work the cross-stitches over two threads of fabric.

BACKSTITCHES (solid red lines on chart): Use one strand of No. 838 dark brown to backstitch the birds at bottom and right. Backstitch the yellow roses with No. 832 medium brass, the white rose with No. 640 dark khaki, and the pink rose with No. 221 dark rose.

Backstitch the birds' eyes using two strands of white.

Press on wrong side. Staple to 11½-inch-square tabletop insert. Mount insert into tabletop following manufacturer's directions, or frame as desired.

COLOR KEY
- ◩ Medium Gold 729
- ◆ Topaz 725
- ⊠ Buttercup 726
- ⊠ Medium Buttercup 727
- ⊡ Yellow 3078
- ▣ Light Yellow 746
- ⊠ Dark Brass 830
- ⊟ Medium Brass 832
- ❋ Light Brass 833
- ⊞ Dark Avocado 935
- ◙ Avocado 3051
- ◐ Medium Avocado 3052
- ⬒ Seafoam 524
- ◪ Dark Green 3345
- ◘ Green 3346

- ⊟ Medium Green 3347
- □ Light Green 3348
- ⊡ Olive Green 734
- ⊡ Dark Blue Green 501
- ▲ Medium Blue Green 503
- ▣ Light Blue Green 504
- ☒ Navy 336
- ⊠ Blue 312
- ◙ Dark Turquoise 517
- ◤ Turquoise 518
- □ Light Turquoise 519
- ⊡ Medium Gray Blue 926
- ◪ Light Gray Blue 927
- ◌ White
- ◼ Black 310

- ⊡ Dark Rose 221
- ◪ Medium Rose 223
- ⊕ Rose 224
- ⊡ Light Rose 225
- ⊙ Red Orange 817
- □ Dark Coral 350
- ⊞ Medium Coral 351
- □ Coral 352
- ⊡ Light Coral 353
- ◪ Peach 754
- ✳ Light Pink 818
- ⊠ Ecru 948
- □ Black-Brown 3371
- ◪ Dark Brown 838
- ◙ Medium Brown 839

- ☐ Tan 841
- ◪ Light Tan 842
- ▣ Dark Khaki 640
- ❒ Khaki 642
- ⊡ Light Khaki 644
- □ Beige 822
- ◉ Dark Gray 844
- ① Gray 645
- ⊞ Medium Gray 647
- □ Light Gray 415
- ◙ Dark Rust 919
- ⊞ Medium Rust 922
- ◪ Light Rust 977
- □ Caramel 437
- ◎ Light Caramel 738

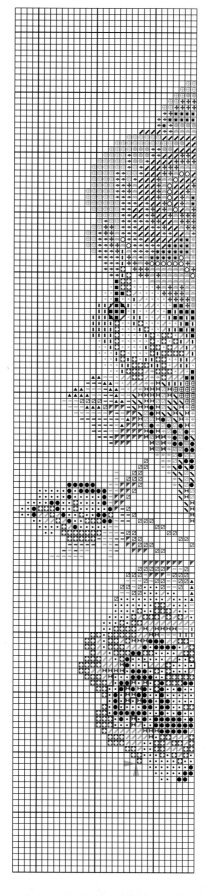

1 Square = 1 Stitch

CIRCLE OF BIRDS TABLE INSERT

MIRROR WITH ROBIN INSERT

Shown on page 67.
Finished size of stitchery is approximately
10½x7½ inches.
Overall size of mirror is 13¼x26 inches with
a 12x9-inch insert for needlework.
Design is 137x93 stitches.

MATERIALS
17½x14½-inch piece of ecru 14-count
    Florina (or Aida) cloth
One skein of DMC embroidery floss in
    colors listed on the color key
Embroidery hoop
Tapestry needle
Masking tape
Hall mirror (available through most
    crafts shops, or by writing to
    Sudberry House, Colton Road, Old
    Lyme, CT 06371)

INSTRUCTIONS
The chart for the mirror insert appears in
two parts at *right*. Shaded rows of stitches
on page 75 represent the overlap of the
two sections. Do not repeat these stitches
when working the design.

Tape raw edges of fabric to prevent
threads from raveling as you work.

The 17½-inch sides of the fabric run
across the top and bottom of the design.
Measure 6 inches up and 4 inches in from
the bottom left corner of the fabric. Begin
working the design here. The starting
point is marked with arrows on the chart
on page 74.

Use two threads of floss to work each
cross-stitch over one square of fabric.

Using two strands of No. 838 dark
brown, make two short straight stitches,
one above the other, for the bird's eye.
After the bird and flower design is
worked, refer to the photo on page 67 and
add a running-stitch border. Using all six

strands of No. 350 red, stitch the border
over two threads and under two threads of
the fabric. The border is stitched six
threads to the outside of the outermost
cross-stitch on all four sides.

Remove tape; press carefully using a
damp cloth and a warm iron.

Mount design on mirror insert board
following manufacturer's suggestions, or
frame as desired.

HEARTH STOOL

Shown on page 66.
Finished size of stitchery is approximately
6½x5½ inches.
Hearth stool is 5½ inches high. Top is 7
inches square.
Design is 93x75 stitches.

MATERIALS
10-inch square of light peach- or blush-
    colored 14-count Aida cloth
DMC embroidery floss in colors listed
    on the color key; number of skeins
    required appears in parentheses
Embroidery hoop
Tapestry needle
Hearth stool (available through crafts
    shops or write to Plain n' Fancy, Inc.,
    P.O. Box 357, Mathews, VA 23109)

INSTRUCTIONS
The chart for the hearth stool appears on
page 76.

Tape raw edges of fabric to prevent
threads from raveling as you work.

Measure down 3 inches and in 3 inches
from the upper left corner of the fabric.
Begin working the design here. The starting point on the chart is marked with blue
arrows.

Use two threads of floss to work each
cross-stitch over one thread of fabric.

continued

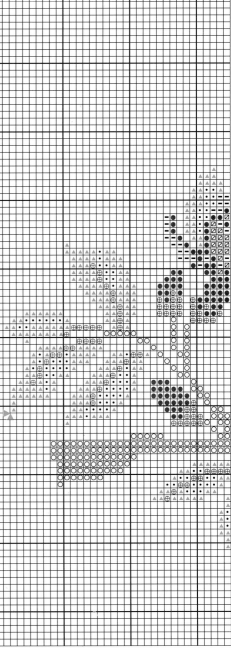

MIRROR WITH ROBIN INSERT

1 Square = 1 Stitch

COLOR KEY
- ☑ Gray 642
- ◎ Brown 780
- ■ Dark Brown 838
- ⊡ Light Green 3347
- ▲ Green 502
- ⊞ Dark Green 520
- ⊡ Orange 971
- ◉ Red 350
- – Pink 352
- ☒ Light Pink 353

SPRINGTIME'S BLESSINGS

DECORATIVE STITCHES: Long stitches are marked on the chart by long red lines that do not necessarily follow the threads of the cloth. Backstitches are marked in short red lines that follow threads of the cloth.

See page 216 for stitch diagrams. Use one strand of floss for working long stitches and backstitches.

Outline the morning glories with backstitches using No. 3685 dark magenta. Use same color for long stitches in the centers of flowers. Begin each center long stitch at flower center. Outline leaves using No. 500 dark green backstitches. Using dark green and long stitches, work veins of the leaves. Outline bird wing and

tail with No. 311 dark blue, and bird body, baby birds, and nest with No. 3371 black-brown.

When stitchery is finished, remove fabric from hoop. Remove tape; press carefully using a damp cloth and a warm iron.

Pad stool top insert and mount design following the manufacturer's directions. Fasten insert into stool.

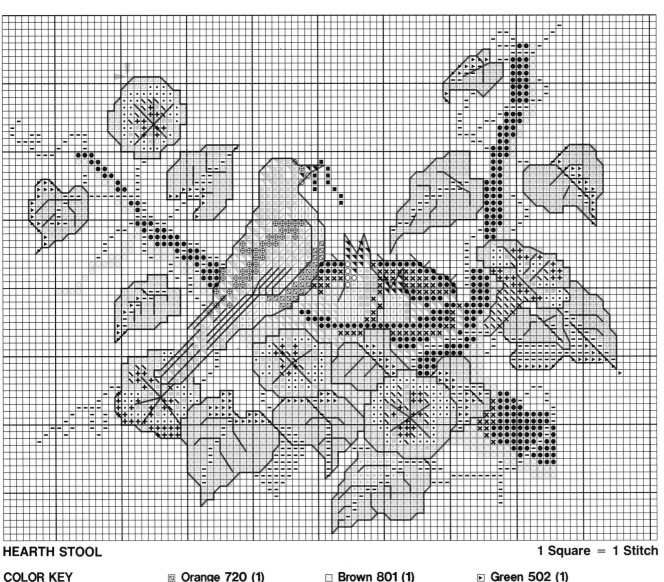

HEARTH STOOL

1 Square = 1 Stitch

COLOR KEY

⊞ Dark Rose 221 (1)	◨ Orange 720 (1)	☐ Brown 801 (1)	▷ Green 502 (1)
☐ Medium Rose 223 (1)	☐ Light Orange 722 (1)	◉ Light Brown 436 (1)	☐ Pale Green 504 (2)
☐ Light Magenta 3609 (1)	◥ Gold 725 (1)	☒ Rust 400 (1)	Dark Blue 311 (1)
☐ Magenta 3608 (1)	◺ Blue 794 (1)	▣ Light Rust 402 (1)	Dark Green 500 (1)
⊞ Lavender 209 (1)	☐ Light Blue 775 (1)	☐ Gray 318 (1)	Dark Magenta 3685 (1)
◎ Pale Peach 951 (1)	☐ Black–Brown 3371 (1)	☐ Light Gray 928 (1)	
	▨ Medium Brown 840 (1)	⊟ Medium Green 501 (1)	

TULIP CURTAINS
AND PLACE MATS

Shown on pages 70 and 71.
Finished size of each tulip design repeat (four tulips in square) is 3⅞x3⅞ inches.
Each tulip design is 55x55 stitches.

MATERIALS
For curtains
Purchased or hand-sewn curtain panels
Fabric and notions required for hand- or machine-sewn curtains, if desired (see instructions)
Length of 8-inch-wide strip of 14-count Aida cloth to fit the running width of the curtain
DMC embroidery floss in colors listed on the color key; number of skeins required will vary depending on width of curtain and number of repeats stitched
Tapestry needle; embroidery hoop

For each place mat
6-inch square of 14-count Aida cloth
One skein of DMC embroidery floss in colors listed on the color key
½ yard of print fabric for place mat top and cording
2 yards of narrow cotton cording
¼ yard of contrasting fabric for ruffle
14½x18-inch piece of muslin for backing
14½x18-inch piece of fleece for interfacing
Tapestry needle
Embroidery hoop

INSTRUCTIONS
Refer to tulip chart, *above right.*

For curtains
Each tulip design repeat measures 3⅞ inches square. The border can be applied to a purchased curtain, or sew your own curtains in the fabric of your choice.

Cross-stitch a length of tulip squares that will fit each curtain panel. *Note:* The border rows on the right side of the first square become the left side border rows for the next square, and so on. Refer to the photo on page 71.

TULIP CURTAINS AND PLACE MAT   **1 Square = 1 Stitch**

COLOR KEY
- ◉ **Dark Pink 892**
- ⊡ **Pink 894**
- ◥ **Yellow 725**
- ⊞ **Dark Green 986**
- ⊠ **Green 987**
- ◼ **Light Green 989**

Use three strands of floss over one thread of fabric to work the cross-stitches.

For hand-sewn curtains
Note: Instructions are for curtains without a ruffle. Adjust length if you make curtains with a ruffle.

Measure the length and the width of the window. Each window will take two finished panels. The length of each piece of fabric should be 8 inches longer than the length of the window.

The total width of the two panels should be 1½ times the width of your window. So, the width of each fabric panel should be one-half of the width of the window times 1½.

Using more fabric than 1½ times the width of your window will make a curtain that is gathered so tightly that the cross-stitch border pattern will be lost in the fabric folds.

Hand- or machine-stitch the border of tulips to the bottom of the curtain. Refer to the photograph on page 71.

Hem sides by folding edge back ¼ inch, then folding again 1 inch, and machine-stitching in place. Machine-stitch a 3-inch hem in the bottom of each panel.

Turn the top of the panel down five inches. Steam-press. Make one machine-stitched line 4¾ inches down from the top edge. Make a second line of stitches 2 inches from the top to form a rod pocket for hanging the curtains.

Piping and ruffles are optional. Curtains can be as tailored or as frilly as you like.

For place mats
TO MAKE THE NAPKIN POCKET: Using three strands of floss over one thread of fabric, work one tulip square for each place mat. Trim the square to leave six
continued

rows of Aida cloth on all sides. Stitch fabric-covered piping on all sides of the square. With right sides facing, sew the stitched square to a matching piece of muslin, leaving an opening for turning; clip seams, turn, and sew opening closed.

TO MAKE THE PLACE MAT: Use ¼-inch seams for all stitching.

Cut fabric, fleece, and muslin backing to measure 14½x18 inches.

Cover 2 yards of cording with place-mat-top fabric. Make a 1-inch ruffle from contrasting fabric. Baste cording and ruffle to place mat top. Machine-stitch cording and ruffle in place.

Hand-stitch tulip pocket in lower right corner of the place mat. Refer to photograph on page 70 for placement. Leave top edge open for napkin or silverware insertion.

Lay place mat top face up on hard surface. Lay muslin, then fleece on top of top fabric. Baste together. Machine-stitch through all layers around outer edge of place mat, leaving an opening along one edge for turning.

Turn right side out. Stitch opening closed. Press place mat.

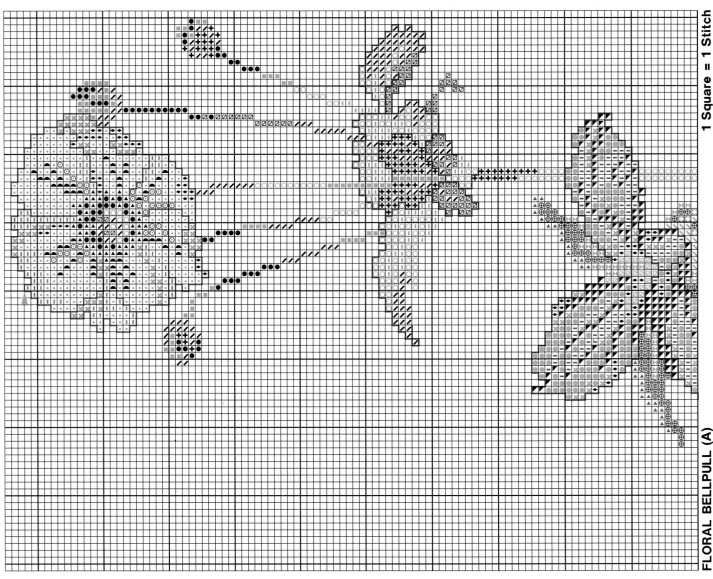

1 Square = 1 Stitch

FLORAL BELLPULL (A)

COLOR KEY

- ▨ Medium Brown 3064
- ◎ Light Gold 3046
- ▢ Dark Yellow 726
- ◪ Medium Yellow 744
- ◯ Light Yellow 727
- ◨ Golden Yellow 3078
- ■ Off White 746
- ◩ Medium Rust 402
- ● Flesh 945
- ⊠ Light Flesh 948
- · Rose 899
- ◧ Medium Rose 3326
- ◫ Light Rose 963
- ▬ Pink 776
- ➤ Light Pink 819
- ⊠ Violet 3041
- ✚ Light Violet 3042
- ◪ Forest Green 500
- ▱ Dark Blue Green 501
- ▬ Blue Green 502
- ◿ Medium Blue Green 503
- ◺ Light Blue Green 504
- ⊞ Seafoam 524
- ⊺ Dark Pistachio 367
- ◿ Medium Pistachio 320
- ◹ Light Pistachio 368
- ◩ Dark Green 469
- ◿ Green 3348
- ◨ Light Green 772
- ◺ Icy Green 966
- ⊞ Avocado 3364
- ▱ Light Avocado 472
- ◪ Celery 369
- ◦ Gray 452
- ✖ Light Gray 453
- ◉ Steel Gray 318
- ▱ Pearl Gray 762
- ▯ White
- ◣ Red – Brown 435
- ◢ Dark Gray 451

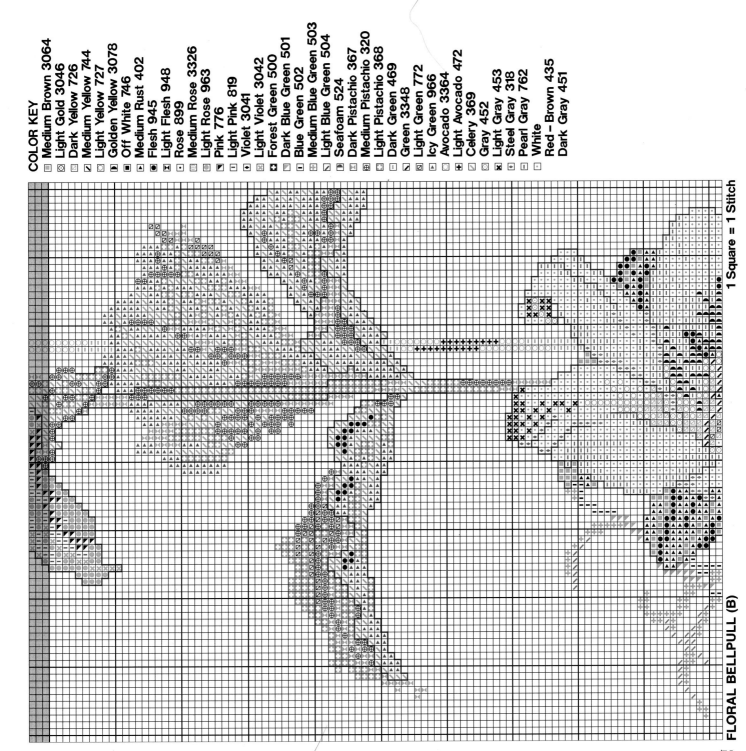

1 Square = 1 Stitch

FLORAL BELLPULL (B)

FLORAL BELLPULL

Shown on page 68.
Finished size is 7x30 inches (excluding tassel).
Design is 77x402 stitches.

MATERIALS
13x36-inch piece of ecru even-weave
    linen with 28 threads to the inch
One skein of DMC embroidery floss in
    colors listed on the color key
½ yard of ecru cotton backing fabric
½ yard of fusible interfacing
Embroidery hoop; tapestry needle

3 yards of cording (optional)
Two 6-inch lengths of 1-inch lattice

INSTRUCTIONS
The complete chart for the bellpull appears in four sections on pages 78–81. Sections B, C, and D each have three shaded rows representing the overlap of each section. Do not rework shaded areas.

Use two strands of floss and work stitches over two threads of fabric.

Using two strands of floss, backstitch as follows: White flowers and butterflies with No. 451 dark gray; pink iris with No. 3041 violet; yellow and pink tulips with No. 435

red-brown; avocado leaves and lighter-colored tulip leaves with No. 469 dark green; pistachio leaves and dark tulip leaves with No. 500 forest green.

Measure 4 inches down from the top and 6½ inches in from the left side. Begin stitching here. (See starting point marked with an arrow on section A on page 78.)

Press finished stitchery on back side.

ASSEMBLY: Cut two pieces of backing each 7½x30½ inches. Fuse backing pieces together using fusible interfacing
continued

1 Square = 1 Stitch

FLORAL BELLPULL (C)

COLOR KEY

▣ Medium Brown 3064
◉ Light Gold 3046
◪ Dark Yellow 726
◪ Medium Yellow 744
◔ Light Yellow 727
◩ Golden Yellow 3078
▪ Off White 746
▲ Medium Rust 402
◕ Flesh 945
⊠ Light Flesh 948
· Rose 899
▦ Medium Rose 3326
◻ Light Rose 963
◪ Pink 776
▭ Light Pink 819
◈ Violet 3041
⊠ Light Violet 3042
✚ Forest Green 500
▨ Dark Blue Green 501
─ Blue Green 502
◪ Medium Blue Green 503
▨ Light Blue Green 504
▦ Seafoam 524
⊕ Dark Pistachio 367
▣ Medium Pistachio 320
◪ Light Pistachio 368
▨ Dark Green 469
▲ Green 3348
◻ Light Green 772
⊕ Icy Green 966
◻ Avocado 3364
✚ Light Avocado 472
◉ Celery 369
⊠ Gray 452
✕ Gray 453
◆ Light Gray 453
▪ Steel Gray 318
▯ Pearl Gray 762
  White
  Red – Brown 435
  Dark Gray 451

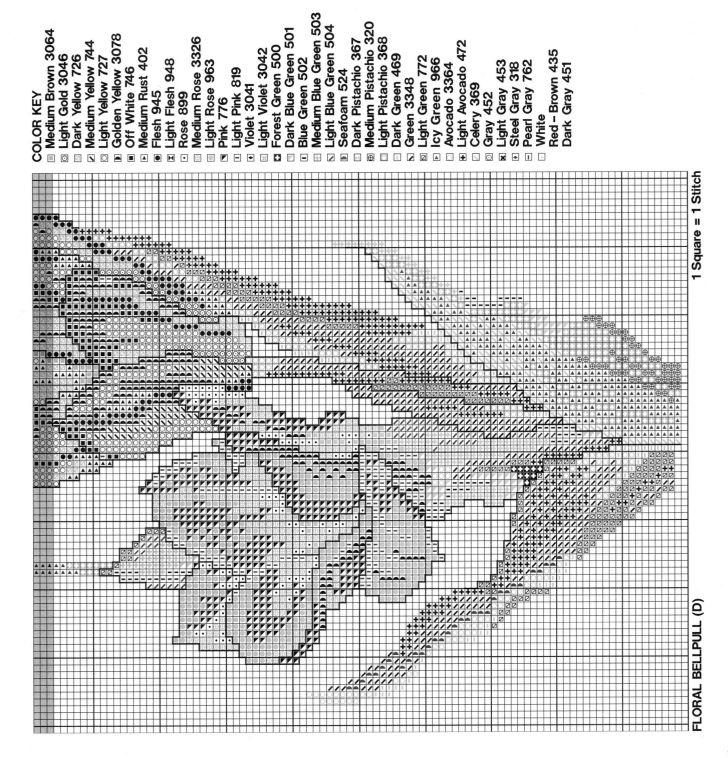

1 Square = 1 Stitch

FLORAL BELLPULL (D)

and following the manufacturer's directions. Using two pieces of backing will help the bellpull hang straight.

Trim stitchery to 7½x30½ inches leaving an equal number of unstitched rows at the top and bottom of the design.

With right sides facing and using ¼-inch seams, machine-stitch together two sides of the finished stitchery and backing fabric.

Cut a 10-inch length of handmade or purchased cording for the hanger. (See instructions for making cording, *below*.) Insert ends of piece of cording for hanger between top of front and back pieces with raw ends against side seams and even with raw edges of fabric at top. Stitch across top edge through fabric and cording ends. Trim seams; turn right side out. Turn raw edges of bottom of bellpull inward and hand-stitch together.

Cover each piece of lattice with backing fabric. Hand-tack one piece across the top of the bellpull and the second piece along the bottom edge to give added weight so the bellpull will hang straight.

Hand-stitch purchased or handmade cording in place. Beginning at the center of the bottom edge, leave 6 inches of cording hanging. Hand-sew the cording around the bellpull, stopping again at the center of the bottom. Leave an additional 6 inches of cording on that end also. Unravel the ends of the cording to form the tassel. Wrap some threads tightly around the top of the tassel to hold it securely.

TO MAKE CORDING: To make cording shown on page 68 you will need 6 balls of DMC No. 5 pearl cotton in assorted pastel colors. Cut strands 1½ times the circumference of the project. The bellpull measures 74 inches around. Cut cotton into 111-inch lengths. Cut 100 strands. Keep the strands taut. Divide the strands into two equal bundles of 50 strands each.

Place a kitchen chair upside down on the table. Tie the end of each bundle over one chair leg. Keep bundles separated.

Holding the ends of one bundle taut and at full distance from the chair, turn bundle of strands to the right to coil threads together. Twist tightly to the kinking point. Twist the second bundle to the right. Take both ropes in one hand, side by side, and wind together to the left.

They will coil to form a thick cording, approximately ½ inch in diameter. The tension created by twisting the thread bundles right, then left, will keep the threads from unraveling. Tape the ends to ensure they do not untwist.

JEWELRY BOX WITH MONOGRAM

Shown on page 69.
Finished size of design is 9¼x6½ inches.
Design is 93x131 stitches.

MATERIALS
11x13 inches of pink 14-count Aida cloth
One skein of DMC embroidery floss in colors listed on the color key
Jewelry box with approximately a 10x7-inch opening for needlework (available through local crafts shops, or write to Sudberry House, Colton Road, Old Lyme, CT 06371)
Embroidery hoop
Tapestry needle

INSTRUCTIONS
The chart for the chest insert appears at *right* and *opposite*. Use the alphabet on the sampler pattern on pages 34 and 35. Center desired initial in the middle of the oval.

With the 13-inch length of fabric running across the top and bottom, measure 3 inches down and 3 inches in from the upper left corner of the fabric. Begin stitching here. The arrow on the pattern shows you where to start.

Use three strands of floss to work cross-stitches over one thread of fabric. Back-stitch stems using two strands of dark green floss. Steam-press the finished stitchery on the wrong side. Mount in box following manufacturer's instructions.

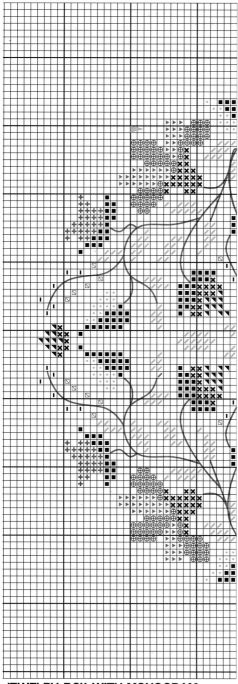

JEWELRY BOX WITH MONOGRAM

1 Square = 1 Stitch

COLOR KEY

◤ Orange 350
⊠ Dark Rose 600
⊡ Rose 603
◺ Yellow Green 907
⊟ Dark Green 704

▣ Green 700
◉ Dark Blue 517
⊞ Blue 807
⊕ Dark Gold 782
▶ Gold 725
⊠ Brown 433

Easter Gifts for A Wonderful Somebunny

Celebrate the joy of Easter morning by surprising little ones with handmade toys and gifts that will captivate their hearts.

Protect your littlest bunny's Easter clothes from that chocolate treat with one of the colorful bibs, *left.* You can brighten a purchased bib with the child's name and a rabbit's favorite treat—carrots. Or, you can combine your needlework with bright-colored bunny buttons.

Children of all ages will fall in love with the irresistible stuffed bunny, *opposite.* The 20-inch doll is made of unbleached muslin adorned with yarn and your needlework, and then dressed in pleated blue Aida cloth overalls featuring—what else?—cross-stitched carrots.

Instructions for these projects begin on page 92.

Maypole Dancing— Memories of Childhood

Surprise a friend—young or old— with a cross-stitched gift that celebrates the ancient custom of honoring the goddess of flowers, the coming of spring, and the first day of May.

Spring flowers in the May basket, *above,* secretly left on a friend's doorstep bring back memories of May Days gone by. Just cover the container of your choice with a border of 2⅛-inch-wide perforated paper decorated with cross-stitched May Day flowers.

The under-and-over motion of the Maypole dance—ribbons weaving and children laughing—sets the scene for the frivolity in the stitchery, *opposite.* The 9½x8-inch design, worked on light green Aida cloth, features skipping children from around the world doing the dance in celebration of winter's departure.

Instructions begin on page 97.

Great Gifts for Mom and Dad

As you were growing up, Mom and Dad always said their favorite gifts were the ones you made yourself. Why stop making them now?

If your mother is a cross-stitcher, she'll love the floss organizer, *above.* Just cover a standard three-ring notebook with your finished stitchery and drapery fabric. For storing extra floss, fill the notebook with plastic pencil cases that have zippers and binder holes.

Mom will also love the floral purse or sweater, *opposite.* The 9-inch-square purse is worked with pearl cotton on needlepoint canvas and given a special touch with a leather back. Using waste canvas and pearl cotton, you can transform any purchased even-weave cotton sweater with at least 10 stitches to the inch into a wonderful Mother's Day gift and a beautiful coordinate to the handbag.

Instructions begin on page 100.

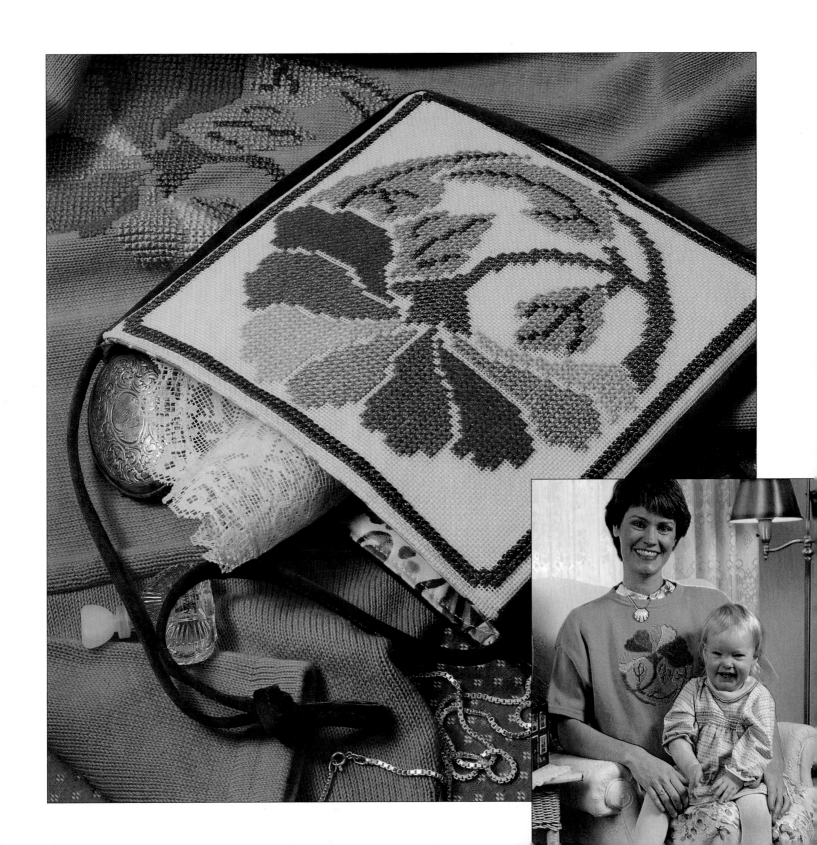

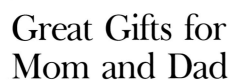

Great Gifts for Mom and Dad

Fair winds, warm seas, and clear skies will be with the sailor who receives one of your nautical wall hangings for Father's Day.

When the summer winds and waters are reaching their prime, give the seaman in your life a Father's Day gift of one of the nautical scenes on these pages. Each is perfect for the boat, but also can be hung proudly in a den or office.

Stitched on light blue hardanger, the 9½-inch-diameter porthole, *left,* circles two sailboats and a lighthouse. The "Adjust Our Sails" message, *opposite, top,* is not only good philosophy for sailing, but also for life. Worked on ecru Aida cloth, the finished stitchery is 6¼x10⅜ inches. The rustic "Bless This Boat" wall hanging, *opposite, bottom,* is worked on light blue hardanger. Finished size is 9x7¾ inches. Personalized with your family name, the stitchery will be displayed proudly on any boat—large or small.

Instructions for these projects begin on page 105.

EASTER BUNNY

Shown on page 85.
Finished height of bunny is 20 inches.

MATERIALS
For the bunny
⅝ yard of 45-inch-wide unbleached
   muslin
4x5-inch piece of 14-count waste canvas
One skein each of DMC embroidery
   floss in colors listed on the color key
13 yards of worsted-weight oatmeal yarn
   (bangs and tail)
1 yard of 1½-inch-wide green check
   ribbon (bow)
Tapestry needle
Embroidery hoop
Polyester fiberfill

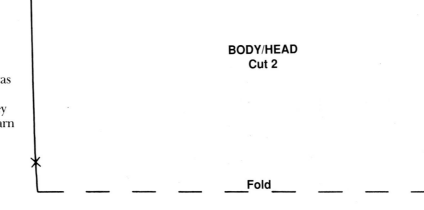

continued

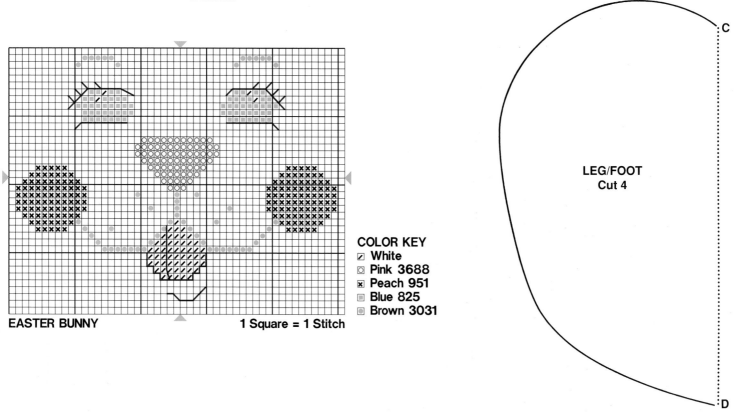

EASTER BUNNY   **1 Square = 1 Stitch**

COLOR KEY
☑ White
◎ Pink 3688
⊠ Peach 951
▣ Blue 825
▨ Brown 3031

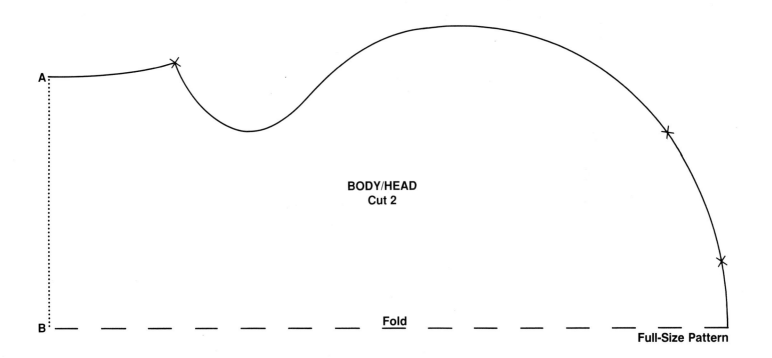

BODY/HEAD
Cut 2

A

B — — — — — — — **Fold** — — — — — —

Full-Size Pattern

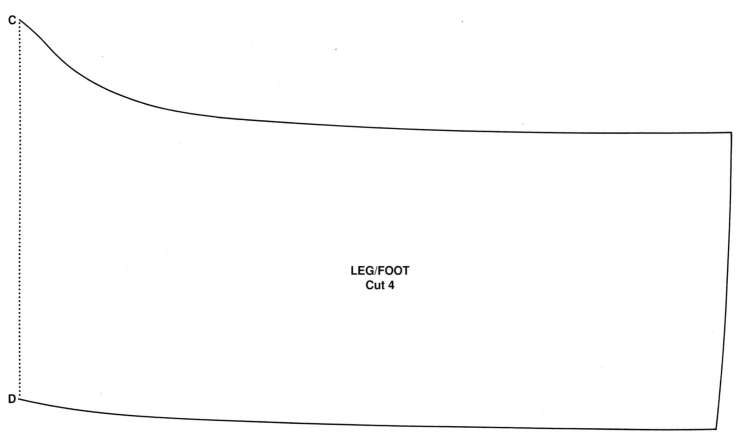

C

LEG/FOOT
Cut 4

D

Full-Size Pattern

For the pants

18x5-inch piece of blue 14-count Aida
   cloth (pants)
Two 10½x2¾-inch strips of blue Aida
   cloth (suspenders)
One skein of DMC embroidery floss in
   colors listed on the color key
Tapestry needle; embroidery hoop
2 small bunny buttons
Tracing paper
Water-erasable pen
Graph paper

INSTRUCTIONS
General

The full-size bunny and pants patterns on
pages 92–96 include ¼-inch seam allowances. Sew all seams with right sides of
fabric facing.

The body, leg, and ear patterns are divided into two pieces each on two pages.
Trace these patterns onto tracing paper
aligning the letter markings to make one
pattern for each piece. Cut out the paper
patterns.

For the bunny

TO STITCH THE FACE: Trace one of
the body/head piece on the unbleached
muslin; do not cut out fabric.

Cut waste canvas to fit the head shape.
Center and baste the canvas to the head.
Position fabric in hoop. Locate center of
head and center of face pattern on page
92; begin working the cross-stitches here.
Arrows on the chart mark the center.

Work cross-stitches using two strands
of floss over one square of waste canvas.

Outline eyes, mouth, and chin with
backstitches using one strand of No. 3031
brown. See stitch diagram on page 216.

When stitching is completed, trim the
waste canvas ¼ inch past the stitching.
Dampen the stitchery with warm water;
gently pull threads of canvas from beneath the stitches; allow fabric to dry.

Press stitched body/head piece on
wrong side of fabric. Cut out. Cut a second body/head piece for the back.

TO ASSEMBLE THE BUNNY: Cut out
all remaining pieces from muslin.

Sew legs, arms, and ears together in
pairs leaving openings for turning. Clip
curves; turn right side out. Press flat.

Firmly stuff arms and legs with polyester fiberfill, leaving about 1 inch unstuffed
at openings.

Sew arms and legs between the X markings on the front piece of the body. Fold
ears in half lengthwise and sew them be-

tween the Xs on the head, placing the fold
of each ear toward the center. Stitch body
front to body back leaving opening along
one body side.

Clip curves; turn body right side out.

Stuff head and body piece; hand-sew
the opening closed.

Cut twelve 6-inch lengths of yarn. Ar-
range strands into one bundle and wrap
center of bundle tightly with thread. Tack
to top center of head to form bangs. Trim
as desired.

For the pants

The chart for the carrots on the pants is
located on page 96. (*Note:* Carrots face to
the outside of the pants.) Use graph paper
to chart the mirror image of the pattern
for the opposite side of the pants' front.

Lay Aida cloth flat. Use the full-size pattern on page 96 to determine your mea-
surements. Using a ruler and water-
erasable pen, and marking out from the
center, mark points A–C along the top of
each half of the fabric.

From solid line A, measure down 3¼
inches and in ¾ inch. Begin stitching the
tip of the inside carrot here. An arrow on
the chart shows you where to begin.

continued

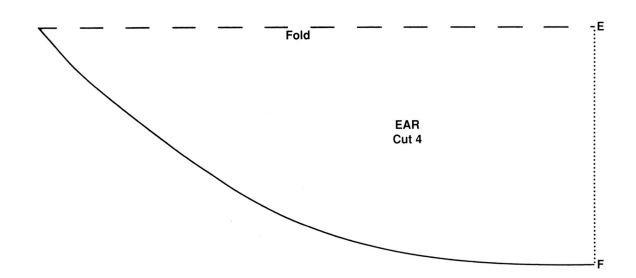

Fold

EAR
Cut 4

E

F

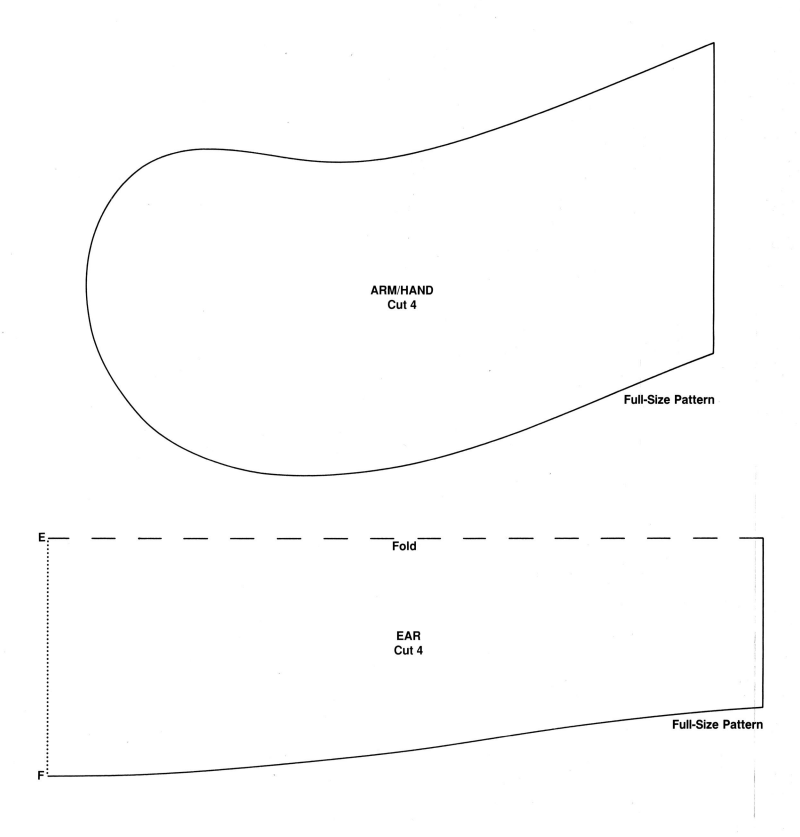

ARM/HAND
Cut 4

Full-Size Pattern

E — — — — — — — — — Fold — — — — — — — — —

EAR
Cut 4

Full-Size Pattern

F

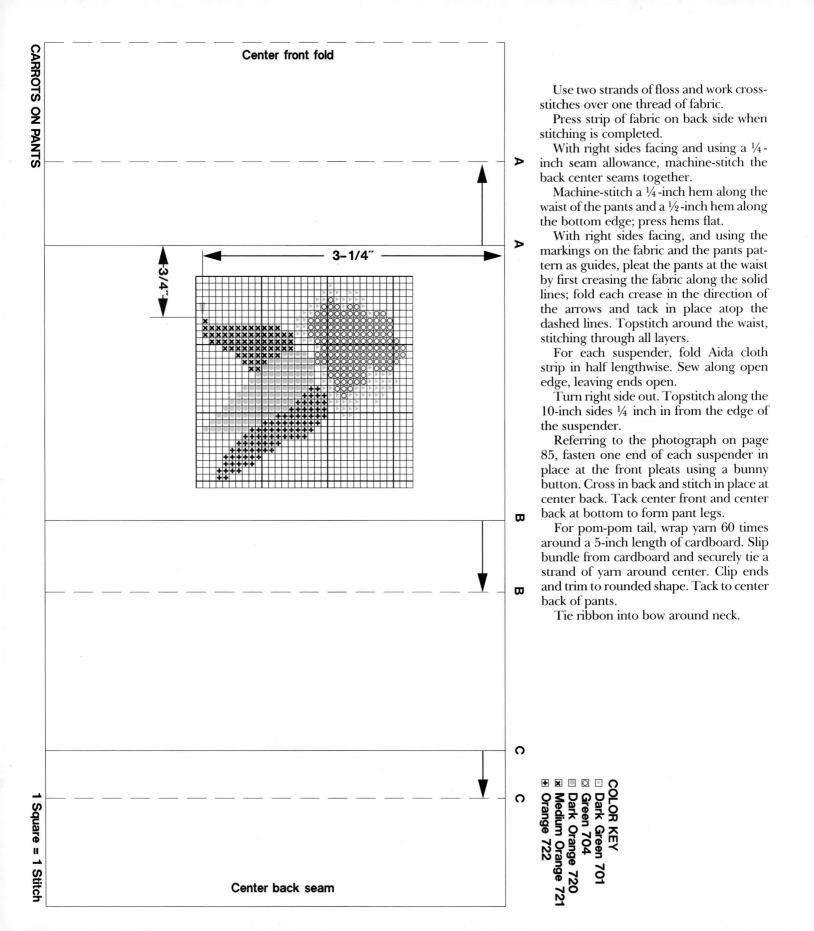

CARROTS ON PANTS

Center front fold

3-1/4"

3/4"

A

A

B

B

C

C

1 Square = 1 Stitch

Center back seam

Use two strands of floss and work cross-stitches over one thread of fabric.

Press strip of fabric on back side when stitching is completed.

With right sides facing and using a ¼-inch seam allowance, machine-stitch the back center seams together.

Machine-stitch a ¼-inch hem along the waist of the pants and a ½-inch hem along the bottom edge; press hems flat.

With right sides facing, and using the markings on the fabric and the pants pattern as guides, pleat the pants at the waist by first creasing the fabric along the solid lines; fold each crease in the direction of the arrows and tack in place atop the dashed lines. Topstitch around the waist, stitching through all layers.

For each suspender, fold Aida cloth strip in half lengthwise. Sew along open edge, leaving ends open.

Turn right side out. Topstitch along the 10-inch sides ¼ inch in from the edge of the suspender.

Referring to the photograph on page 85, fasten one end of each suspender in place at the front pleats using a bunny button. Cross in back and stitch in place at center back. Tack center front and center back at bottom to form pant legs.

For pom-pom tail, wrap yarn 60 times around a 5-inch length of cardboard. Slip bundle from cardboard and securely tie a strand of yarn around center. Clip ends and trim to rounded shape. Tack to center back of pants.

Tie ribbon into bow around neck.

COLOR KEY
▷ Dark Green 701
▷ Green 704
◎ Dark Orange 720
▣ Medium Orange 721
⊞ Orange 722
⊠

BABY BIBS

Shown on page 84.

MATERIALS

Purchased baby bib with insert for cross-stitch (available at most crafts stores)
One skein of DMC embroidery floss in colors listed on the color key
Tapestry needle
3 bunny-shaped buttons
Graph paper

INSTRUCTIONS

The prefinished bibs shown on page 84 are manufactured by the Janlynn Corporation, 34 Front Street, Indian Orchard, MA 01151.

Ceramic bunny buttons are from A Homespun Heart, 810 Bluffwood Drive, Iowa City, IA 52245.

For the bib with bunny buttons

Measure down 22 threads and in 4 threads from the upper left corner of the Aida fabric pocket on the bib. Begin stitching the left end of the row of carrots from the chart, *right*. An arrow on the chart marks the beginning stitch. Use two strands of floss and work cross-stitches over one thread of fabric.

Make two long stitches for carrot tops using two strands of No. 701 green. (See stitch diagrams on page 216.)

When all stitching is complete, carefully press the bib with a damp cloth and warm iron.

Sew bunny buttons in place, referring to the photograph on page 84.

(*Note:* If you are using ceramic buttons like the ones shown on page 84, hand washing is required.)

For the bib with carrots and baby's name

Use the alphabet on the sampler pattern on pages 36 and 37 to personalize the bib with the baby's name. Use the carrot pattern on the bunny's pants pattern, *left*. (*Note:* The carrots on the bib on page 84 have been flopped to face the outside of the bib.) Plan the pattern on graph paper; the length of the child's name will alter the center of the finished design.

Graph the name three squares to the right of the bunch of carrots. When charting is completed, locate the center of the pattern and the center of the bib pocket. Begin stitching here.

Using two strands of floss, work all cross-stitches over one thread of fabric.

When all stitching is completed, press the bib with a damp cloth and warm iron.

MAYPOLE DANCE WALL HANGING

Shown on page 87.
Finished size of stitchery is 9½x8 inches.
Design is 134x111 stitches.

MATERIALS

16-inch square of light green 14-count Aida cloth to double-mat as shown
One skein of DMC embroidery floss in colors listed on the color key
Tapestry needle
Embroidery hoop

INSTRUCTIONS

The chart for the design appears on pages 98 and 99. It is divided into two sections. Work all of the section on page 98 first, then finish with page 99. Three shaded rows of stitches on page 99 represent the overlap of the two sections. Do not repeat these stitches when working the design.

Hem or tape the raw edges of the fabric to prevent threads from raveling.

Measure down 4 inches and in 8 inches from the top left corner of the fabric. Begin stitching the top stitch of the Maypole here. Use three strands of floss and work cross-stitches over one thread of fabric.

continued

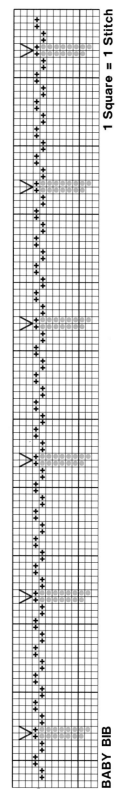

1 Square = 1 Stitch

BABY BIB

COLOR KEY
▨ Orange 720
⊞ Green 701

MAYPOLE DANCE WALL HANGING

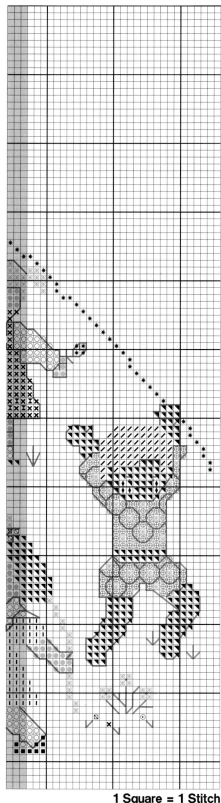

1 Square = 1 Stitch

COLOR KEY
- ◌ White
- ⊙ Rust 920
- ⊡ Tan 738
- ◥ Brown 433
- ⊞ Light Brown 3064
- ☑ Black–Brown 3371
- ■ Dark Gray 413
- ▥ Light Gray 414
- ⊠ Gold 742
- ◺ Yellow 744
- ▯ Blue 312
- ⊞ Light Blue 334
- ▧ Dark Purple 550
- ⊕ Medium Purple 209
- − Light Purple 210
- ✻ Dark Rose 600
- ◪ Rose 603
- ▨ Red 349
- ✕ Pink 899
- ▦ Teal 943
- ⊠ Green 905
- ⊡ Light Green 704

Decorative stitches

When all cross-stitches are completed, work backstitches and French knots using two strands of floss. (Stitch diagrams appear on page 216.)

BACKSTITCHES (red lines on diagram): Use No. 433 brown to outline boy's face and hands (upper left); Indian girl's hands; blond girl's hair (upper right); Oriental boy's hands and feet; the Dutch girl's shoes; hair, hands, and face of girl in sailor dress.

Use No. 3064 light brown to outline girl's hands, tummy, and face (far left); Dutch girl's face and hands; Oriental boy's face and basket; blond girl's face, hands, and legs (upper right).

Use No. 3371 black-brown to outline boy's face, hair, hands, tummy, and legs (bottom right); boy's hair and shoes (upper left).

Use No. 600 dark rose for all mouths; No. 433 brown for all eyebrows and noses; and No. 3371 black-brown for Indian girl's and Oriental boy's eyes.

Use No. 742 gold for trim on Oriental boy's red jumpsuit, and No. 550 dark purple for details on purple dress, apron, and hat, and for design on purple shorts and shirt.

Use No. 312 blue to outline collar of blue sailor dress, blue pants, baseball cap, and Indian girl's dress and boots.

Use No. 413 dark gray to outline boy's gray pants and collar, and tennis shoes of girl in baseball cap and socks of girl in sailor dress. Use No. 603 rose to outline pink jumper and white blouse. Use No. 600 dark rose to outline girl's pink sweatshirt. Use No. 349 red to outline socks and stitch detail on shoes of girl in baseball cap.

Outline purple tulip with No. 550 dark purple, and pink tulips with No. 600 dark rose. Backstitch stems on flowers and grass with No. 905 green. Backstitch stems of tiny flowers in front with No. 704 light green.

FRENCH KNOTS (red dots on chart): Using only one strand of floss, use No. 312 blue to make French knot eyes on the blond girl (upper right), girl in baseball cap, and Dutch girl.

Use No. 433 brown to make French knot eyes on boy (upper left) and girl (lower right).

Use No. 3371 black-brown to make French knot eyes on Indian girl and navel on tummy and eyes of boy (far right).

Use No. 433 brown to make three French knot buttons on each shoe of Dutch girl.

Use No. 3064 light brown to make a navel on girl's tummy (far left).

Make French knot centers on yellow flowers with one strand of No. 433 brown. Make French knots on lavender flowers (except tulip) with No. 550 dark purple.

Use No. 312 blue to make French knot fringe at collar and bottom of Indian girl's dress.

Make a French knot using No. 349 red under the backstitch on each mouth except for the girl in baseball cap. Use No. 600 dark rose to make French knot centers for the flowers in boy's hand (upper left) and for pink flowers in the grass under the Maypole.

TO FINISH: Lightly press finished stitchery on back side. Frame as desired.

FLOWER BASKET BORDER

Shown on page 86.
Finished depth of band is 2⅛ inches.
Design is 30 stitches deep.

MATERIALS

4-inch-wide strip of ecru perforated paper long enough to go around container of your choice
One skein of DMC embroidery floss in colors listed on the color key
Tapestry needle
Purchased basket or other container
White crafts glue

INSTRUCTIONS

Measure the circumference of the basket, flowerpot, canister, or other container you wish to decorate. *Note:* The container must have straight sides for the band to lie flat. Cut the perforated paper the length of the circumference plus 2 inches for overlapping.

The design for the border is *below* and *opposite.* Three shaded rows of stitches represent the overlap of the two sections. Do not repeat these stitches when working the design. Center the large flower basket motif horizontally and vertically on the strip of perforated paper.

Repeat the grid and small clusters of flowers as needed to fill the length of the strip of paper.

Diagrams for all stitches appear on page 216. Be careful not to pull stitches too tightly or the paper will tear.

Use two strands of floss to work cross-stitches over one square of paper.

Use two strands of No. 825 blue and the running stitch to work grid background over one square and under one square of paper. Use one strand of No. 825 blue to backstitch bow. Backstitch stems on plum buds with one strand of No. 943 green.

Backstitch light green leaves with one strand of No. 943 green, and pink flowers with one strand of No. 891 red.

Use one strand of No. 801 brown for French knot centers on yellow flowers.

When stitching is complete, trim paper, leaving one row of squares above and below the design. Wrap the paper around the container, overlap ends, and glue the band onto the back of the container.

FLORAL PURSE

Shown on page 89.
Finished size of purse is 9 inches square.
Design with border is 70x70 stitches.

MATERIALS

12-inch square of yellow 16-mesh needlepoint canvas
One skein of DMC No. 5 pearl cotton in colors listed on the color key
Tapestry needle
12-inch square of cream-colored fabric
12-inch square of fusible webbing paper
One 9½-inch square and one 1½x27-inch strip of pigskin or synthetic suede
1 yard of medium-weight fusible woven interfacing
⅓ yard of lining fabric
Coordinating thread
Large snap

INSTRUCTIONS

The chart for the purse is located *opposite.* Locate the center of the design and the center of the needlepoint canvas. Arrows on the chart mark the horizontal and vertical centers. Begin stitching here.

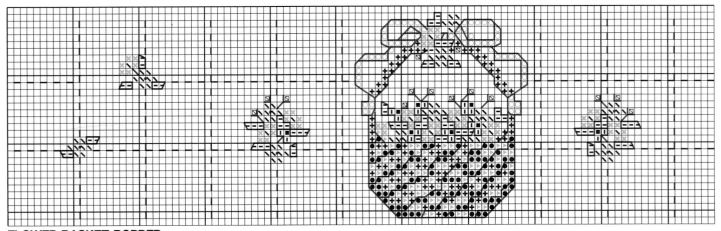

FLOWER BASKET BORDER

COLOR KEY	
☐ Light Blue 827	☑ Rose 894
⊟ Light Green 993	◉ Brown 801
☒ Purple 340	⊞ Old Gold 729
◩ Plum 718	☐ Rust 301
▣ Red 891	◹ Yellow 742

Blue 825
Green 943

Use two strands of pearl cotton and work cross-stitches over one thread of canvas.

When design is complete, block canvas to restore original shape.

Use the fusible webbing paper to fuse the cream-colored fabric to the wrong side of the cross-stitched canvas. This will prevent the lining from showing through the unworked canvas when the purse is finished. (Follow manufacturer's directions on fusible webbing.)

Trim canvas and cream-colored interfacing ½ inch beyond outside row of stitched border. (Total trimmed measurement is 9½ inches square.)

Cut one 9½-inch square of fusible interfacing and one 1½x27-inch strip of fusible interfacing. Fuse to wrong side of leather pieces. *Note:* Test a sample by fusing interfacing to a scrap of leather. Too much steam may cause shrinking.

Cut two 9½-inch-square pieces of lining fabric for front and back and one 1½x27-inch piece of lining fabric for boxing strip.

With right sides facing, sew boxing strip to purse front leaving top edge free and using ¼-inch seams. Repeat to join boxing strip to purse back.

continued

FLORAL PURSE/SWEATER

1 Square = 1 Stitch

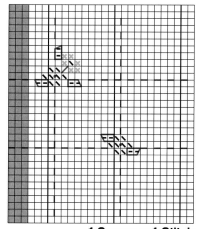

1 Square = 1 Stitch

COLOR KEY

⊞	Teal 991	⊠	Aqua 597
▶	Dark Green 367	⊡	Peach 353
◎	Light Green 368	⊙	Purple 553
		⊠	Pink 602

Sew lining pieces in same manner, leaving an opening in one boxing seam along the bottom of the purse for turning after the lining is attached to purse. With right sides facing and boxing strip seams matched, sew lining to purse around top edge using ¼-inch seams.

Turn lining right side out. Slip-stitch opening closed. Slip lining into purse. With transparent nylon thread, topstitch close to top seam through all thicknesses.

Center and stitch one half of snap closure to front lining and one half to back lining at top edge of bag.

FLORAL SWEATER

Shown on page 89.
Finished size of stitchery is 8x8 inches.
Design is 62x62 stitches.

MATERIALS

Purchased even-weave cotton sweater with 10 or more knitted stitches to the inch
10-inch square of No. 8 waste canvas
One skein of No. 5 DMC pearl cotton in colors listed on the color key
Tapestry needle

INSTRUCTIONS

Determine desired placement of design on sweater. *Note:* The neckline of the sweater chosen will determine where you wish to begin. The center blue petal on the flower design on the sweater shown on page 89 begins 2½ inches below the center of the neckline. Baste the waste canvas to the sweater front.

Cross-stitch the design according to the chart on page 101, eliminating the two border rows. Use two threads of pearl cotton over one thread of canvas.

When cross-stitch is complete, remove basting stitches from waste canvas. Carefully trim away canvas around design. According to manufacturer's instructions, dampen waste canvas and pull threads from design.

"DECORATE WITH STITCHES" FLOSS ORGANIZER

Shown on page 88.
Finished book as shown measures 9x11½ inches. Design measures 7¾x10⅜ inches. Design is 86x114 stitches.

MATERIALS

15x18-inch rectangle of ecru 11-count Aida cloth
One skein of DMC embroidery floss in colors listed on the color key
Gold metallic thread
Embroidery hoop; tapestry needle
Purchased scrapbook or photograph album with ring binder
½ yard of cotton drapery fabric for back, binding, spine, flaps, and lining
½ yard of fleece
3 yards of narrow piping
Plastic pencil cases with zippers and holes to fit binder

INSTRUCTIONS

Hem or tape the raw edges of the Aida cloth to prevent threads from raveling.

The chart for the design appears *opposite*. Measure 3½ inches down and 3½ inches in from the upper left corner of the fabric; begin stitching the top left flower here. An arrow on the chart shows you where to begin.

Use three strands of floss and work cross-stitches and backstitches over one thread of fabric.

When all cross-stitching is complete, work decorative stitches as follows. See stitch diagrams on page 216.

BACKSTITCHES (red lines on chart): Backstitch the "Decorate with Stitches" message with one strand of No. 333 dark purple.

FRENCH KNOTS (shaded red squares on chart): Work cross-stitches first according to symbols. Then, using one strand of gold metallic thread, make French knots over cross-stitches in flower centers and on flower buds.

TO FINISH BOOK COVER: Remove tape from edges of fabric. Press the piece on the back side using a warm iron and a damp cloth.

Draw three rectangles on brown paper. Draw one the size of one cover, another the size of the spine, and the third the length of the front cover but just five inches wide (inner flap). Add ½-inch seam allowances to patterns; cut out.

From the cotton drapery fabric, cut one large rectangle for the back cover; cut the cross-stitched front the same size. Cut one spine and two flaps from the cotton fabric. Cut matching shapes from fleece.

Baste fleece pieces to wrong sides of corresponding drapery fabric pieces.

Sew piping to *each* long edge of the spine piece. With right sides together, sew album front and back pieces to spine using ¼-inch seam allowances.

From the cotton drapery fabric, cut lining to match the assembled cover.

On one long side of *each* inner flap piece, press under ¼ inch twice; machine-hem. With right sides together and raw edges even, sew piping around assembled cover. With right sides facing, sew flaps to ends of fabric covers.

Pin right side of lining atop wrong sides of flaps. Sew lining (through all thicknesses) atop the piping seam, leaving an opening for turning. Clip the corners, turn the piece to the right side, and press; slip-stitch the opening closed. Slip flaps over album cover. Insert plastic cases.

COLOR KEY
⊠ Dark Green 561
◩ Medium Green 562
⊠ Light Green 563
▢ Dark Purple 333
⊟ Medium Purple 340
▣ Light Purple 341
⊞ Dark Pink 3607
◨ Medium Pink 3608
▢ Light Pink 3609
▶ Plum 917
▪ Dark Aqua 958
◧ Aqua 959
▥ Salmon 3378
⊞ Dark Gold 783
⊟ Gold 725
◙ Gold Metallic Thread

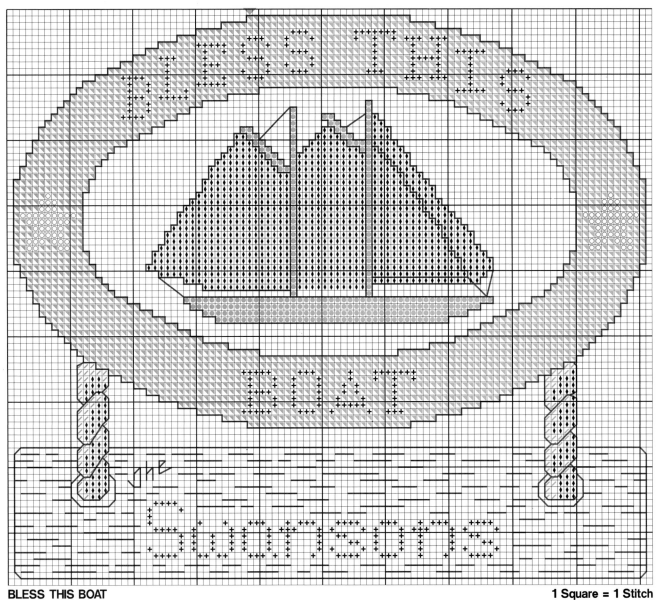

BLESS THIS BOAT

1 Square = 1 Stitch

COLOR KEY

◫ White (1)	⊞ Red 817 (1)
◓ Ecru 739 (1)	◉ Dark Brown 632 (1)
◪ Tan 437 (1)	Medium Brown 434 (1)
◥ Blue 311 (2)	Black-Brown 3371 (1)

"BLESS THIS BOAT" WALL HANGING

Shown on page 91.
Finished stitchery is 9x7¾ inches.
Design is 100x86 stitches.

MATERIALS

15x14 inches of light blue hardanger
  fabric
DMC embroidery floss in colors listed
  on the color key; number of skeins
  required appears in parentheses
Tapestry needle
Embroidery hoop

INSTRUCTIONS

The chart for the design is *opposite*.

Hem or tape raw edges of fabric to prevent threads from raveling as you work. Use two strands of floss and work all cross-stitches over two threads of fabric.

Measure 3½ inches down and 6½ inches in from the top left corner of the cloth. Begin stitching the design here. An arrow on the chart marks the starting point. Stitch diagrams appear on page 216.

Use your favorite alphabet or the Wedding Sampler alphabet on page 115 to personalize the wall hanging.

continued

COLOR KEY
⊞ Dark Gray 451
⊠ Gray 453
◥ Light Gray 762
⊠ Dark Blue 312
⦿ Blue 775
⊞ Sea Green 926
◳ Light Sea Green 828
▣ Brown 839
⊠ Light Brown 841
▱ Beige 3033
▦ Red-Brown 632
▨ Red 347
▢ Dark Green 367
☑ Green 368
  Black–Brown 3371

ADJUST OUR SAILS

1 Square = 1 Stitch

BACKSTITCHES (red lines on chart): Work backstitches over two threads as follows: Using two strands of No. 3371 black-brown, work all backstitches on the sailboat and stitch the word "The" on the signboard.

Backstitch the grain in the wood on the sign and outline the sign and the rope with two strands of No. 434 medium brown. Backstitch the inside and outside of the blue oval with No. 311 blue.

TO FINISH: Remove tape from the edges of fabric. Press stitchery on the back side, using a damp cloth and warm iron. Frame as desired.

BACKSTITCHES (red lines on chart): See stitch diagrams on page 216. Use two strands of No. 535 dark gray over two threads for all backstitches in the scene inside of the porthole. Backstitch the porthole with two strands of No. 780 rust.

FRENCH KNOT: Use one strand of No. 437 brown to make a doorknob on the lighthouse door.

TO FINISH: Remove tape from edges of fabric. Press stitchery on back side, using a damp cloth and warm iron. Frame as desired. (The circular frame shown has an inside diameter of 12 inches.)

BACKSTITCHES (red lines on chart): See stitch diagrams on page 216. When all cross-stitching is complete, work backstitches over two threads as follows: Using two strands of No. 3371 black-brown, backstitch around the sailboat, lighthouse, foliage, rocks, and waves.

Backstitch the lettering using two strands of No. 312 dark blue.

TO FINISH: Remove tape from edges of fabric. Press stitchery on back side, using a damp cloth and warm iron. Frame cross-stitch as desired.

PORTHOLE WITH SAILBOATS

Shown on page 90.
Finished stitchery is 9½ inches in diameter.
Design is 104x105 stitches.

MATERIALS
15-inch square of light blue hardanger fabric
DMC embroidery floss in colors listed on the color key; number of skeins required appears in parentheses
Tapestry needle
Embroidery hoop

INSTRUCTIONS
The chart for the porthole design is located *opposite*.

Hem or tape raw edges of fabric to prevent threads from raveling as you work. Use three strands of floss and work all cross-stitches over two threads of fabric.

Measure 3 inches down and 7 inches in from the top left corner of the cloth. Begin stitching the top of the porthole here. An arrow on the pattern shows you where to begin stitching.

When all cross-stitching is complete, work decorative stitches as follows.

"ADJUST OUR SAILS" WALL HANGING

Shown on page 91.
Finished size of stitchery is 6¼x10⅜ inches.
Design is 69x113 stitches.

MATERIALS
13x17 inches of ecru 11-count Aida cloth
One skein of DMC embroidery floss in colors listed on the color key
Tapestry needle
Embroidery hoop

INSTRUCTIONS
The chart for the design is located on page 105.

Hem or tape raw edges of fabric to prevent threads from raveling as you work. Use three strands of floss and work all cross-stitches over one thread of fabric.

Measure 3½ inches down and 4 inches in from the top left corner of the cloth. Begin stitching the top left corner of the design here. Arrows on the pattern show you where to begin.

COLOR KEY
☐ White (1)
⊞ Light Gray 842 (1)
⊠ Gray Brown 840 (1)
☑ Gray 453 (1)
⊕ Brown 437 (1)
▣ Light Brown 438 (1)
● Dark Gold 729 (2)
⊠ Gold 676 (2)
Ⅰ Light Gold 677 (2)
◪ Blue 806 (1)
▶ Green 320 (1)
◉ Barn Red 347 (1)
✳ Red 350 (1)
   Dark Gray 535 (1)
   Rust 780 (1)

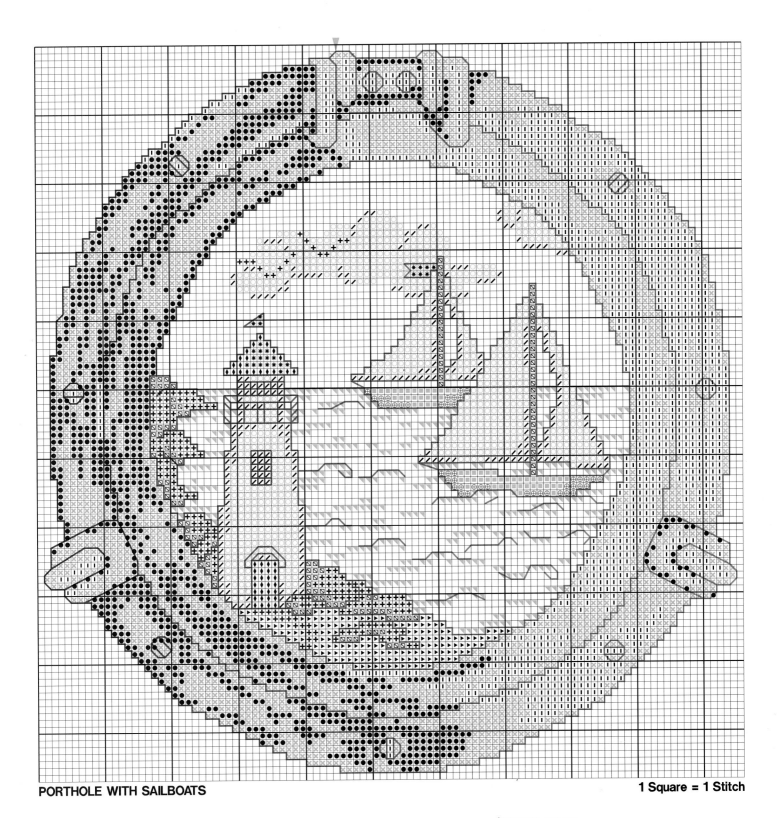

PORTHOLE WITH SAILBOATS

1 Square = 1 Stitch

Romantic Notions for a Pastel Wedding

When the voice of the heart speaks above all others and daydreams become reality, only the finest wedding gifts and accessories will do. Beribboned with tender sentiment, the versatile basket of flowers appears on the sampler as well as the bride's sweater on page 111.

Names and dates are etched forever on keepsake projects shown here and on the following pages.

The pillow design, *right,* is stitched on hardanger fabric and ruffled in a glorious yellow floral chintz.

When the bridal bouquet is dried and put away for tomorrow's memories, the posies in the basket, *opposite,* will remain in glorious bloom for eternity. A border of hearts and flowers neatly frames the recording of this romantic event.

Patterns and instructions for these projects begin on page 112.

Romantic Notions for a Pastel Wedding

Among the important items a bride must attend to are place cards for the head table, gifts for the bridesmaids, and her honeymoon wardrobe.

The diminutive sachet, *above,* is a romantic presentation of motifs borrowed from the wedding sampler. It makes a charming gift for bridal attendants and requires only a small amount of stitching time.

Perforated paper place cards, beautifully lettered in cross-stitch, add to the elegance of the head table at the reception.

A purchased cotton sweater, *opposite,* is a great background for a floral pattern. Choose a sweater in an even-weave fabric for uniform cross-stitches. The sweater shown has six threads per inch and uses five strands of floss for solid coverage.

Instructions begin on page 112.

PLACE CARDS

Shown on page 110.
Finished size is 4½x2 inches.

MATERIALS

4½x4 inches of ecru perforated paper
    for each card
One skein of DMC embroidery floss in
    colors listed on the color key
Tapestry needle

INSTRUCTIONS

Use the heart and leaf motif on the pillow pattern on page 114 and the alphabet on page 115. Refer to the photograph on page 110 for placement.

Fold paper to measure 4½x2 inches. Plan your place card first on graph paper. Chart the names you want to use on the paper. Then, center the heart and leaf design seven rows below the bottom of the capital letter of the name.

Center the design on the paper and begin working the capital letter of the name three rows below the folded edge of the paper. Use three strands of floss for cross-stitches. Use two strands of No. 434 rust brown to backstitch names. Work stitches over one square of paper.

WEDDING SACHET

Shown on page 110.
Finished size of design is 4 inches square.
Design is 41x40 stitches.

MATERIALS

7-inch-square piece of hardanger fabric
One skein each of DMC embroidery
    floss in colors listed on the color key
¼ yard of fabric for backing and ruffle
⅔ yard of cording
Polyester fiberfill
Embroidery hoop; tapestry needle

INSTRUCTIONS

The chart for the sachet is located at the top of page 115.

Hem or tape raw edges of fabric to prevent threads from raveling as you work. Locate the center of the hardanger and the center of the design. Arrows on the chart mark the center. Begin stitching here.

Use three strands of floss to work the cross-stitches over two threads of fabric. Backstitch around flower with two strands of No. 3685 burgundy. (*Note:* Backstitched areas are indicated by red lines on the chart.)

When the sachet top is finished, remove the tape. Press the stitchery carefully on the wrong side using a damp cloth and warm iron.

Finish sachet as desired.

WEDDING SAMPLER

Shown on page 109.
Finished size of design is 7x10 inches.
Design is 77x115 stitches.

MATERIALS

15x18 inches of hardanger
DMC embroidery floss in colors listed
    on the color key; number of skeins
    required appears in parentheses
Tapestry needle; embroidery hoop
Graph paper

INSTRUCTIONS

Chart date and names on a sheet of graph paper using the letters and numbers provided on page 115. (Refer to the chart, *opposite,* for placement. Center names and date within the space allowed.)

Hem or tape raw edges of fabric to prevent threads from raveling as you work. Measure 4 inches down and 4 inches in from the top left corner of the cloth. Begin stitching the upper left corner heart of the border here. Use three strands of floss for cross-stitches and two strands for backstitches. Work all stitches over two threads of fabric. (*Note:* Backstitched areas are indicated by red lines on the chart.)

Backstitch "and" and "were married on" with No. 370 gold.

Backstitch corner hearts and all flowers with No. 3685 burgundy, names and date with No. 434 rust brown, basket and basket handle with No. 928 gray, and bow on handle with No. 958 dark blue-green.

Remove tape from finished stitchery; press on wrong side using a damp cloth and warm iron. Frame as desired.

KEEPSAKE PILLOW

Shown on page 108.
Finished size of design is 7x7 inches.
Design is 77x77 stitches.

MATERIALS

13-inch-square piece of hardanger fabric
One skein of DMC embroidery floss in
    colors listed on the color key
¾ yard of fabric for backing and ruffle
1 yard of cording
Polyester fiberfill
Embroidery hoop; tapestry needle
Graph paper

INSTRUCTIONS

The chart for the pillow is located on page 114. Chart the date and names on a sheet of graph paper using the letters and numbers provided on page 115. (Refer to the chart on page 114 for placement.)

Hem or tape raw edges of fabric to prevent threads from raveling as you work. Measure 3 inches in from the left side of the fabric and 3 inches down from the top of the fabric; begin stitching the top left corner of the border here.

Use three strands of floss for cross-stitches and two strands for backstitches. Work stitches over two threads of fabric. (*Note:* Backstitched areas are indicated by red lines on the chart.)

Backstitch flowers and hearts with No. 3685 burgundy and names and date with No. 434 rust brown.

When the pillow top is finished, remove the tape. Press the stitchery carefully on the wrong side using a damp cloth and warm iron. Finish pillow as desired.

COLOR KEY

- ▶ Magenta 718 (1)
- ⊞ Rose 603 (1)
- ◲ Pink 963 (1)
- ◼ Dark Green 699 (1)
- ◻ Medium Green 904 (2)
- ◩ Light Green 704 (1)
- ◣ Dark Blue Green 958 (1)
- ⊟ Light Blue Green 964 (1)
- ⊕ Purple 792 (1)
- ◩ Gray 928 (1)
- ⊡ Light Gray 926 (1)
- ⊠ Gold 370 (1)
  - Burgundy 3685 (1)
  - Rust Brown 434 (1)

WEDDING SAMPLER

1 Square = 1 Stitch

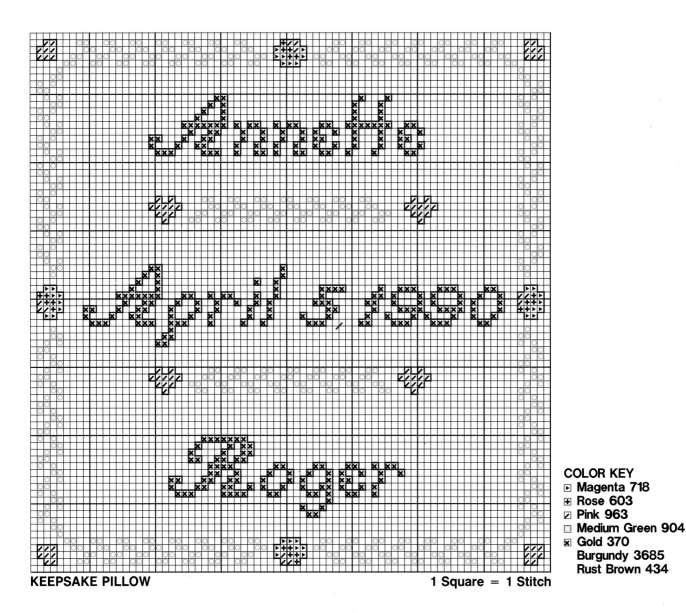

COLOR KEY
- ▶ Magenta 718
- ⊞ Rose 603
- ☑ Pink 963
- ☐ Medium Green 904
- ⊠ Gold 370
-    Burgundy 3685
-    Rust Brown 434

KEEPSAKE PILLOW   1 Square = 1 Stitch

FLOWER BASKET COTTON SWEATER

Shown on page 111.
Finished size of design is 11x6 inches.
Design is 65x48 stitches.

MATERIALS
Purchased sweater with approximately
  six threads per inch (We used a
  cotton crew from Eddie Bauer.)
One skein each of DMC embroidery
  floss in colors listed on the color key
Tapestry needle

INSTRUCTIONS
The basket pattern for the sweater is borrowed from the sampler pattern on page 113. (See photograph on page 109.)

Locate the center of the front of the sweater. Measure down 3 inches from the neckline. Begin stitching the knot of the blue bow here.

Use the stockinette (even-weave) stitches of the knitted fabric as the grid to work the cross-stitches just as you would use even-weave threads on cross-stitch fabric.

Use five strands of floss for cross-stitches and work each stitch over one knit-stitch of fabric. (*Note:* No backstitches are worked on the sweater.)

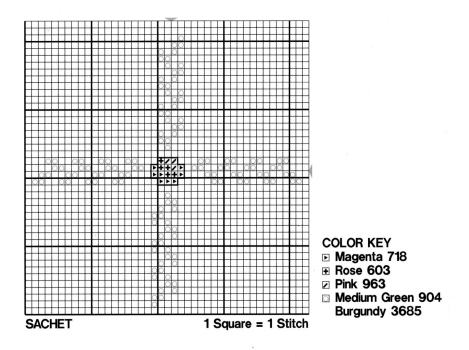

SACHET

1 Square = 1 Stitch

COLOR KEY
- ▶ Magenta 718
- ⊞ Rose 603
- ◪ Pink 963
- ☐ Medium Green 904
  Burgundy 3685

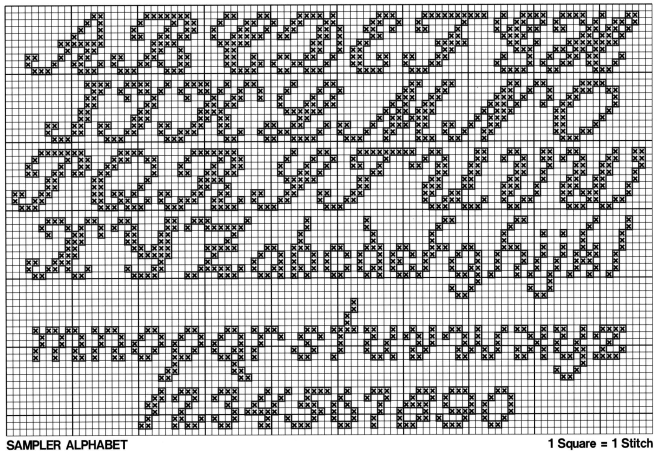

SAMPLER ALPHABET

1 Square = 1 Stitch

For Sunny Days
SUMMER PLEASURES

Mary isn't the only one who gets pleasure from a wonderful row of summer flowers in her nursery-rhyme garden. Pack a lunch and treat yourself to a picnic among the posies. No need to invite the ants. They'll come anyway.

With jonquils and pansies, the showy summer garden wall hanging, *right,* explodes with spectacular color. The design worked on 14-count Aida cloth measures 38x12 inches.

Use individual flowers or groups of blossoms to make pillows and trim linens.

Instructions begin on page 122.

*From the delicate lily of the valley to the
dewy petals of the rose, summer flowers
provide an ever-changing palette of color
for needlecrafters.*

Small floral motifs used in the projects, *above,* work equally well alone or in multiples. Dramatic purple linen combined with waste canvas makes a handsome background for the bouquet of designs plucked from the seven patterns available on pages 132 and 133. Each motif is 30 stitches square, so it's easy to mix and match.

Even-weave tablecloth fabric that comes with woven square grids is perfect for using one or all of these pretty designs. Or, coordinate hand towels with a bathroom wallpaper or fabric. Worked on purchased towels with an insert of 12-count fabric, the finished projects make lovely last-minute gifts.

Salute the summer with this spectacular tablecloth, *opposite,* featuring a rose wreath center. Stitched over four threads of 28-count linen, the cloth is deserving of the finest summer garden party.

Instructions for the picture frame mat are on page 125. Instructions for the towels and tablecloths begin on page 131.

FRUIT AND VEGETABLES
BASKETS TO FILL
FOOD IS FOR SHARING
LOVE AND GOODWILL

Gathering baskets and bowls full of fruits, vegetables, and berries is a gardener's delight. Cross-stitchers, too, can harvest lots of wonderful design ideas from summer's bounty.

The garden sampler, *opposite,* produces an abundance of opportunities for all kinds of kitchen gifts. Worked on 16-count peach Aida cloth, it draws inspiration from a Saturday morning farmers' market or a country roadside stand bursting with baskets of freshly picked produce.

An ever-popular design motif, the strawberry works well on fingertip towels and gift bags, *above.* Tuck a jar of your best homemade strawberry jam in the bag and you've got a gift that's a sure winner.

Patterns and instructions for these projects begin on page 133.

121

FLORAL WALL HANGING

1 Square = 1 Stitch

FLORAL WALL HANGING

Shown on pages 116 and 117.
Finished size of design area is 38x12 inches.
Design is 531x168 stitches.

MATERIALS
49x21-inch piece of 14-count Aida fabric
DMC embroidery floss in colors listed
  on the color key; number of skeins
  required appears in parentheses
Embroidery hoop; tapestry needle

INSTRUCTIONS
The chart for the sampler is divided into sections and printed on pages 122–130.

Shaded areas on the charts show you where one section overlaps with the next. Do not rework the shaded areas as you move from section to section. These areas are only placement guides.

On pages 126 and 128, the sections of the pattern are too deep to fit on one page. The lettering has been repeated on the right-hand page to allow you to easily finish that section.

Use three strands of floss and work the cross-stitches over one thread of fabric.

Backstitch areas indicated by solid red lines with two strands of No. 642 tan.

Measure 4½ inches down from the top and 7 inches in from the left side; begin stitching here. The arrow on the first section of the chart on page 122 indicates the beginning stitch. Mount fabric in hoop and cross-stitch all letters and flower motifs from left to right.

Steam-press finished stitchery on the wrong side.

Frame the sampler as desired.

Note: Individual flowers or groups of flowers in this design will make beautiful pillows, table linens, and other decorating accessories.

When you pull one flower from the design, fill in the shapes of leaves or petals that are covered by other flowers or leaves to complete the blossom you have chosen.

COLOR KEY
- White (1)
- Beige 822 (1)
- Gray 3072 (1)
- Aqua 959 (1)
- Medium Aqua 991 (2)
- Dark Aqua 924 (2)
- Periwinkle 333 (2)
- Medium Periwinkle 340 (2)
- Light Periwinkle 341 (1)
- Violet 553 (1)
- Dark Lavender 208 (1)
- Medium Lavender 209 (1)
- Light Lavender 210 (1)
- Canary Yellow 972 (1)
- Lemon Yellow 445 (1)
- Yellow 3078 (1)
- Light Yellow 745 (1)
- Dark Terra-Cotta 221 (1)
- Terra-Cotta 356 (2)
- Dark Coral 350 (1)
- Medium Coral 352 (1)
- Light Coral 353 (1)
- Orange 608 (1)
- Bittersweet 721 (2)
- Red 817 (1)
- Avocado 471 (1)
- Olive 522 (3)
- Light Olive 524 (2)
- Sea Foam 562 (1)
- Moss Green 580 (1)
- Bright Green 701 (1)
- Chartreuse 703 (1)
- Pistachio 890 (1)
- Hunter Green 895 (1)
- Dark Parrot Green 905 (1)
- Parrot Green 906 (2)
- Forest Green 989 (1)
- Cream 712 (1)
- Black 310 (1)
- Tan 642 (1)

FLORAL WALL HANGING

1 Square = 1 Stitch

COLOR KEY
- ◨ **White (1)**
- ⊠ **Beige 822 (1)**
- ☑ **Gray 3072 (1)**
- ▶ **Aqua 959 (1)**
- ◩ **Medium Aqua 991 (2)**
- ◻ **Dark Aqua 924 (2)**
- ◥ **Periwinkle 333 (2)**
- ◪ **Medium Periwinkle 340 (2)**
- ⊡ **Light Periwinkle 341 (1)**
- ◫ **Violet 553 (1)**
- ⊠ **Dark Lavender 208 (1)**
- ◗ **Medium Lavender 209 (1)**
- ☑ **Light Lavender 210 (1)**
- ◻ **Canary Yellow 972 (1)**
- ◘ **Lemon Yellow 445 (1)**
- ◫ **Yellow 3078 (1)**
- ◻ **Light Yellow 745 (1)**
- ◲ **Dark Terra-Cotta 221 (1)**
- ◉ **Terra-Cotta 356 (2)**
- ◉ **Dark Coral 350 (1)**
- ◉ **Medium Coral 352 (1)**
- ◻ **Light Coral 353 (1)**
- ◣ **Orange 608 (1)**
- ◻ **Bittersweet 721 (2)**
- ⊠ **Red 817 (1)**
- ◨ **Avocado 471 (1)**
- ◻ **Olive 522 (3)**
- ◻ **Light Olive 524 (2)**
- ☑ **Sea Foam 562 (1)**
- ◧ **Moss Green 580 (1)**
- ▥ **Bright Green 701 (1)**
- ◲ **Chartreuse 703 (1)**
- ◻ **Pistachio 890 (1)**
- ⊞ **Hunter Green 895 (1)**
- ⊟ **Dark Parrot Green 905 (1)**
- ▧ **Parrot Green 906 (2)**
- ◼ **Forest Green 989 (1)**
- ◻ **Cream 712 (1)**
- ◻ **Black 310 (1)**
-   **Tan 642 (1)**

LILY OF THE VALLEY AND PRIMROSE MAT

Shown on page 118.
Finished mat before framing is 12x14½ inches.

MATERIALS
16x18-inch piece purple linen
16x18-inch piece 12-count waste canvas
DMC embroidery floss in colors listed on the color key (*Note:* For the frame shown, you need two skeins of dark parrot green, No. 905. One skein of all other colors is sufficient.)
16x18-inch piece of fleece
16x18-inch piece backing fabric
30 inches of piping
Water-erasable marker
Tapestry needle
Embroidery hoop

INSTRUCTIONS
These instructions are for mat shown on page 118. The mat shown uses the lily of the valley and the primrose charts on page 132. Size of mat and opening may be adjusted by changing number of motifs. Any combination of flower motifs may be used to complement your own decorating scheme.

Baste waste canvas to linen. The 16-inch measurement is along the top and bottom of the rectangle. The rectangle is 18 inches down each side. Measure down 2½ inches from the top and 3 inches in from the left side of the fabric. Begin marking the blocks here. Refer to the position guide diagram on page 132. Using the grid lines on the waste canvas as a guide, use the water-erasable marker to mark four 30-stitch-square blocks across

the top and bottom and five blocks down each side. This leaves a center area that measures approximately 5x7½ inches inside the stitching.

The flower charts on pages 132 and 133 are on 30-square grids. This allows for the exact positioning of each flower within the squares on the waste canvas.

Cross-stitch all motifs using three strands of floss over one square of waste canvas. When stitchery is complete, remove the basting threads and carefully cut away the unworked canvas, leaving ½ inch of canvas around the stitching. Follow manufacturer's instructions for removing waste canvas threads.

Carefully press back side of stitchery.

Cut away the inside opening and the outside edges one inch from the cross-stitches. You will now have a mat that measures 12x14½ inches before framing.

From fleece, cut a matching piece to fit the mat; baste to wrong side. With right sides facing, and using ¼-inch seams, sew piping to inside opening of mat.

Cut backing to measure same size as mat. With right sides together, and using ¼-inch seams, sew backing to mat along piping stitches. Trim linen, backing, and fleece ⅛ inch from piping sewing line.

Turn backing to back side of mat. Press mat flat. Frame as desired.

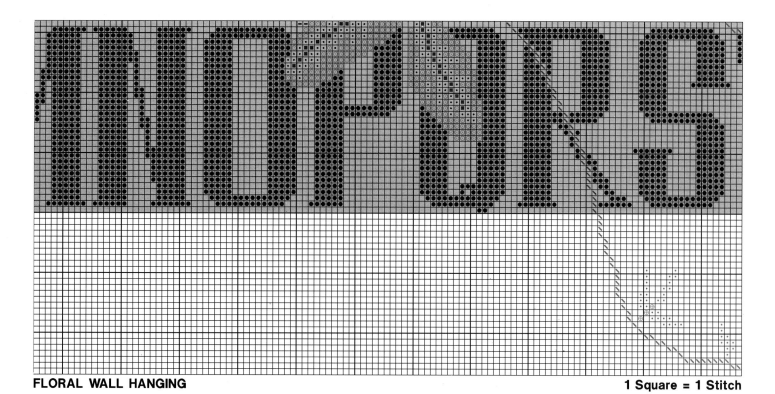

FLORAL WALL HANGING

1 Square = 1 Stitch

COLOR KEY

◫ White (1)
⊠ Beige 822 (1)
◲ Gray 3072 (1)
▸ Aqua 959 (1)
▣ Medium Aqua 991 (2)
◨ Dark Aqua 924 (2)
◥ Periwinkle 333 (2)
◉ Medium Periwinkle 340 (2)
⊡ Light Periwinkle 341 (1)
◼ Violet 553 (1)
⊠ Dark Lavender 208 (1)
◐ Medium Lavender 209 (1)
◱ Light Lavender 210 (1)

◹ Canary Yellow 972 (1)
◘ Lemon Yellow 445 (1)
▦ Yellow 3078 (1)
◻ Light Yellow 745 (1)
◺ Dark Terra-Cotta 221 (1)
◉ Terra-Cotta 356 (2)
◉ Dark Coral 350 (1)
◎ Medium Coral 352 (1)
▢ Light Coral 353 (1)
◸ Orange 608 (1)
◻ Bittersweet 721 (2)
⊠ Red 817 (1)
⊞ Avocado 471 (1)
⊡ Olive 522 (3)

◻ Light Olive 524 (2)
◲ Sea Foam 562 (1)
▦ Moss Green 580 (1)
▨ Bright Green 701 (1)
◻ Chartreuse 703 (1)
◘ Pistachio 890 (1)
⊕ Hunter Green 895 (1)
⊟ Dark Parrot Green 905 (1)
▣ Parrot Green 906 (2)
◼ Forest Green 989 (1)
◨ Cream 712 (1)
◘ Black 310 (1)
　 Tan 642 (1)

128

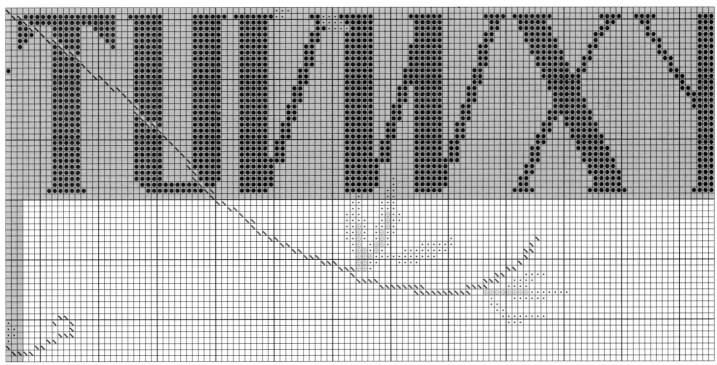

FLORAL WALL HANGING

1 Square = 1 Stitch

COLOR KEY

- ▣ White (1)
- ⊠ Beige 822 (1)
- ▨ Gray 3072 (1)
- ▷ Aqua 959 (1)
- ▣ Medium Aqua 991 (2)
- ▢ Dark Aqua 924 (2)
- ◥ Periwinkle 333 (2)
- ◎ Medium Periwinkle 340 (2)
- ⊡ Light Periwinkle 341 (1)
- ▣ Violet 553 (1)
- ⊠ Dark Lavender 208 (1)
- ▶ Medium Lavender 209 (1)
- ▨ Light Lavender 210 (1)

- ▣ Canary Yellow 972 (1)
- ◨ Lemon Yellow 445 (1)
- ▦ Yellow 3078 (1)
- ▢ Light Yellow 745 (1)
- ◣ Dark Terra-Cotta 221 (1)
- ◉ Terra-Cotta 356 (2)
- ◙ Dark Coral 350 (1)
- ◎ Medium Coral 352 (1)
- ▢ Light Coral 353 (1)
- ◢ Orange 608 (1)
- ▢ Bittersweet 721 (2)
- ⊠ Red 817 (1)
- ⊞ Avocado 471 (1)
- ⊡ Olive 522 (3)

- ▢ Light Olive 524 (2)
- ▨ Sea Foam 562 (1)
- ▣ Moss Green 580 (1)
- ▣ Bright Green 701 (1)
- ⊡ Chartreuse 703 (1)
- ◨ Pistachio 890 (1)
- ⊞ Hunter Green 895 (1)
- ⊟ Dark Parrot Green 905 (1)
- ▣ Parrot Green 906 (2)
- ▣ Forest Green 989 (1)
- ▣ Cream 712 (1)
- ▣ Black 310 (1)
-   Tan 642 (1)

129

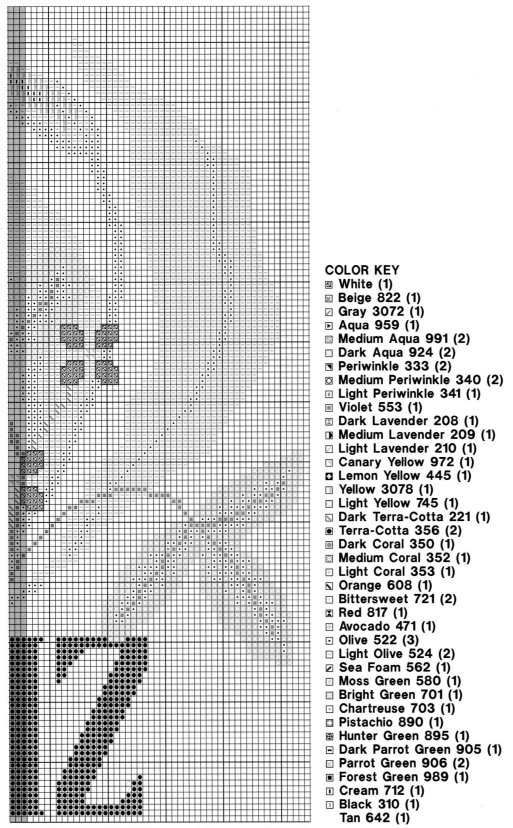

COLOR KEY
◨ White (1)
⊠ Beige 822 (1)
⊡ Gray 3072 (1)
▣ Aqua 959 (1)
▥ Medium Aqua 991 (2)
☐ Dark Aqua 924 (2)
◤ Periwinkle 333 (2)
⊚ Medium Periwinkle 340 (2)
▣ Light Periwinkle 341 (1)
▦ Violet 553 (1)
⊠ Dark Lavender 208 (1)
▶ Medium Lavender 209 (1)
☐ Light Lavender 210 (1)
☐ Canary Yellow 972 (1)
◘ Lemon Yellow 445 (1)
☐ Yellow 3078 (1)
☐ Light Yellow 745 (1)
◣ Dark Terra-Cotta 221 (1)
◉ Terra-Cotta 356 (2)
▤ Dark Coral 350 (1)
◎ Medium Coral 352 (1)
☐ Light Coral 353 (1)
◥ Orange 608 (1)
☐ Bittersweet 721 (2)
⊠ Red 817 (1)
▥ Avocado 471 (1)
⊡ Olive 522 (3)
☐ Light Olive 524 (2)
☑ Sea Foam 562 (1)
☐ Moss Green 580 (1)
▥ Bright Green 701 (1)
☐ Chartreuse 703 (1)
▤ Pistachio 890 (1)
⊞ Hunter Green 895 (1)
⊟ Dark Parrot Green 905 (1)
▥ Parrot Green 906 (2)
▣ Forest Green 989 (1)
⊡ Cream 712 (1)
▥ Black 310 (1)
  Tan 642 (1)

FLORAL WALL HANGING　　1 Square = 1 Stitch

HAND TOWELS

Shown on page 118.

MATERIALS

Purchased towels with even-weave
 inserts for cross-stitch (available at
 needlework stores)
One skein *each* of DMC embroidery floss
 in colors listed on color key
Tapestry needle

INSTRUCTIONS

Note: Towels shown are manufactured by
Charles Craft, P.O. Box 1049, Laurinburg, NC 28352, and can be purchased in
many sizes. The inserts vary in width, but
are always 12 stitches per inch.

Using the photograph on page 118 as a
guide, select desired flower motifs. The
charts are on pages 132 and 133. Work all
cross-stitches using three strands of floss
over one fabric thread.

Mark vertical and horizontal center of
the towel band. Determine the number of
30-stitch-square motifs that will fit onto
band; also determine suitable spacing between the motifs.

Beginning at center of chart and center
of towel insert, stitch motifs across the
band. Press band on wrong side.

FLORAL TABLECLOTH

Shown on page 118.

MATERIALS

14-count even-weave tablecloth fabric
 (available at most crafts stores)
One skein *each* of DMC embroidery floss
 in colors listed on color key
Tapestry needle

INSTRUCTIONS

Any combination of the floral designs on
pages 132 and 133 may be used. Use
three strands of floss to work the cross-
stitches over one thread of fabric.

Cut the fabric to the desired tablecloth
size. Hem. Mark random blocks on the
fabric for placement of the motifs. Stitch
flowers in marked blocks, alternating the
direction the flowers face on the cloth.

ROSE WREATH TABLECLOTH

Shown on page 119.
Finished size of cloth is 31x31 inches.
Wreath motif is 16 inches in diameter.

MATERIALS

35-inch square of 28-count even-weave
 cloth
DMC embroidery floss in colors listed
 on the color key; number of skeins
 required appears in parentheses
White sewing thread; tapestry needle
Masking tape

INSTRUCTIONS

Bind raw edges of cloth with masking tape
to prevent fraying. Refer to chart on page
137. Find center of cloth. Measuring 4
inches down from center, begin cross-
stitching bottom rose using three strands
of floss over four threads of cloth. An arrow indicates the beginning stitch.

Remove masking tape; trim cloth to 32
inches square. Hem; press.

CORRECTING MISTAKES

Regardless of the complexity of a design or of a stitcher's skill, mistakes are
inevitable. What to do about mistakes
depends largely upon their magnitude,
when they're discovered, and what is
necessary to correct them.

Small errors, such as working one or
two additional stitches within a shaded
area or stitching the end of a leaf so
that it points in an opposite direction,
will usually go unnoticed.

Some areas of stitching, however,
must be perfect, or the remainder of
the design won't look right. When
you've stitched around the border of a
sampler, for example, and the corners
don't align, there's little choice but to
find the error and rework the stitches.

To remove stitches, use *sharp* scissors with tiny blades. Working from the
back side, carefully snip away the
threads and discard them. Use tweezers to pluck away stubborn threads.

131

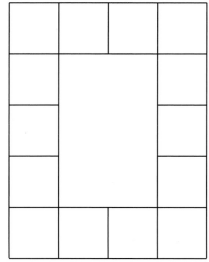

POSITION GUIDE

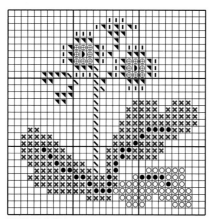

PRIMROSE

COLOR KEY
- ◨ Dark Bittersweet 720
- ⊕ Bittersweet 722
- ⊡ Light Yellow 744
- ◥ Yellow 972
- ◲ Avocado 471
- ⊠ Parrot Green 905
- ◎ Light Parrot Green 907
- ◉ Green 3345

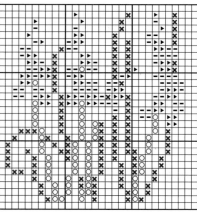

GRAPE HYACINTH

COLOR KEY
- ⊟ Dark Violet 550
- ▶ Violet 553
- ⊠ Parrot Green 905
- ◎ Light Parrot Green 907

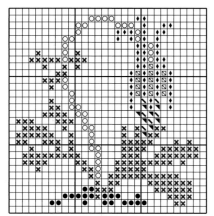

COLUMBINE

COLOR KEY
- ◩ Deep Rose 309
- ◈ Red 498
- ◥ Yellow 972
- ◲ Avocado 471
- ⊠ Parrot Green 905
- ◎ Light Parrot Green 907
- ◉ Green 3345

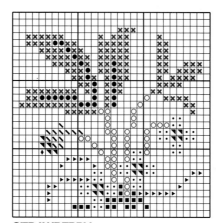

STRAWBERRY

COLOR KEY
- ⊡ White
- ■ Terra–Cotta 355
- ◈ Red 498
- ◥ Yellow 972
- ▶ Violet 553
- ◲ Avocado 471
- ⊠ Parrot Green 905
- ◎ Light Parrot Green 907
- ◉ Green 3345

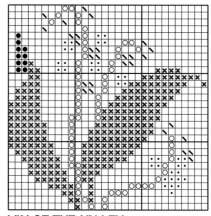

LILY OF THE VALLEY

COLOR KEY
- ⊡ White
- ◲ Avocado 471
- ⊠ Parrot Green 905
- ◎ Light Parrot Green 907
- ◉ Green 3345

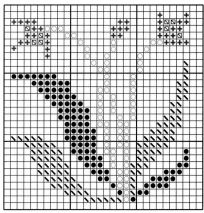

SCILLA

COLOR KEY
- ⊡ Deep Rose 309
- ⊞ Rose 3326
- ◨ Avocado 471
- □ Light Parrot Green 907
- ◉ Green 3345

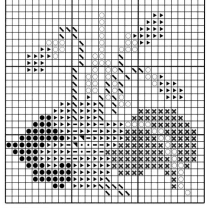

VIOLET

COLOR KEY
- ⊡ White
- ◤ Yellow 972
- ⊟ Dark Violet 550
- ▶ Violet 553
- ◨ Avocado 471
- ⊠ Parrot Green 905
- □ Light Parrot Green 907
- ◉ Green 3345

GARDEN SAMPLER

Shown on page 120.
Finished sampler is 11¼x8¾ inches.
Design is 189x151 stitches.

MATERIALS

15x18-inch piece of 16-count peach
   Aida cloth
DMC embroidery floss in colors listed
   on the color key; number of skeins
   required appears in parentheses
Embroidery hoop
Tapestry needle

INSTRUCTIONS

The garden sampler is divided into four charts that appear on pages 134–136. Shaded areas represent the overlap from one pattern piece to the next. Do not re-stitch these shaded areas.

Measure 3 inches down from top of fabric and 3 inches in from the left side; begin stitching the upper left corner of the design here. An arrow indicates the starting point. Using two strands of floss, work stitches over one thread of fabric.

Press stitchery; frame as desired.

GUEST TOWEL AND GIFT BAG

Shown on page 121.
Finished size of design repeat is 3½x1¾ inches (towel) and 4x3½ inches (bag). Finished size of bag shown is 6½x5 inches, excluding handle.

MATERIALS

One skein *each* of DMC embroidery floss
   in colors listed on the color key
Tapestry needle

For the towel
Fingertip towel with even-weave insert

For the bag
Gift bag designed for cross-stitch with
   14 threads per inch (available in most
   crafts shops)

INSTRUCTIONS
For the towel
Note: The towel shown on page 121 is from Charles Craft, P.O. Box 1049, Laurinburg, NC 28352 and is available through crafts stores. The chart for the strawberries is on the bottom of page 136.

Locate center of even-weave band and center of design; begin stitching here. Disregard shading over some symbols. Use three strands of floss to work cross-stitches over one thread of fabric.

Backstitch flowers with two strands of No. 400 mahogany. Use two strands of No. 310 black to add random French knot seeds on strawberries. Repeat motif, leaving three rows between each design.

For the bag
Note: Bag on page 121 is from Janlynn, 34 Front Street, Indian Orchard, MA 01151, and is available at most crafts stores. Locate center of bag front and center of design; begin stitching here. Do not stitch shaded portion of design on page 136 for bag. Use three strands of floss to work cross-stitches over two threads of fabric.

Backstitch flowers with two strands of No. 400 mahogany. Use two strands of No. 310 black to add random French knot seeds on strawberries. Press carefully.

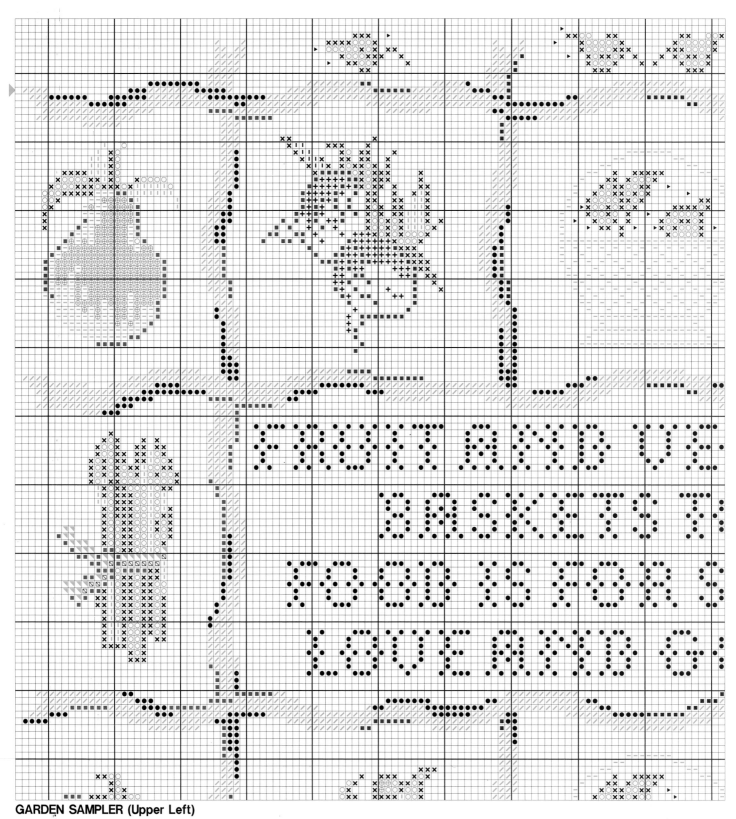

GARDEN SAMPLER (Upper Left)

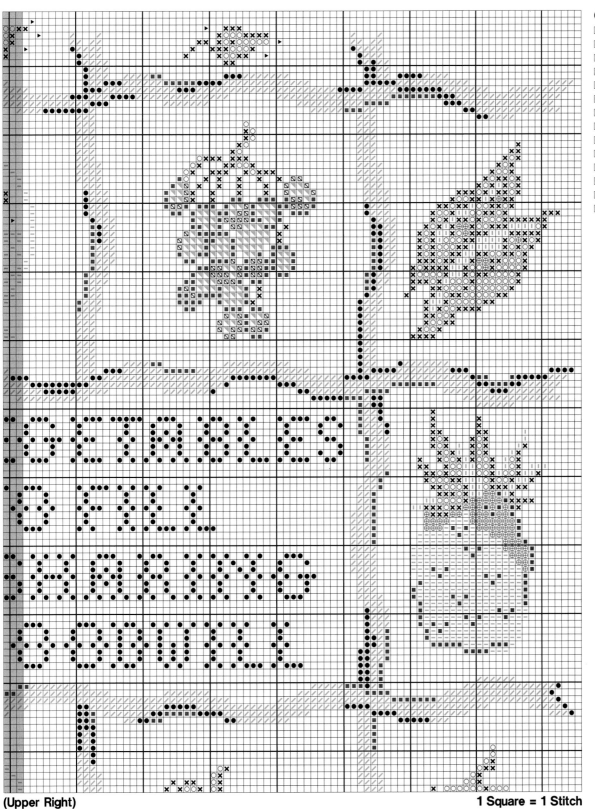

COLOR KEY
- ▣ Navy 939 (1)
- ◉ Medium Blue 930 (1)
- ▨ Light Blue 932 (2)
- ▨ Dark Green 3051 (1)
- ⊡ Medium Green 3052 (1)
- ◎ Light Green 3053 (1)
- ▨ Purple 315 (1)
- ◥ Light Purple 316 (1)
- ⊞ Red 347 (1)
- ⊡ Light Red 3328 (1)
- ⊟ Tan 3045 (1)
- ⊕ Yellow 677 (1)
- ▷ Dark Peach 758 (1)
- ◎ Peach 945 (1)

(Upper Right)

1 Square = 1 Stitch

COLOR KEY

- ◨ Navy 939 (1)
- ◉ Medium Blue 930 (1)
- ◿ Light Blue 932 (2)
- ⊠ Dark Green 3051 (1)
- ⊡ Medium Green 3052 (1)
- ◎ Light Green 3053 (1)
- ◩ Purple 315 (1)
- ◺ Light Purple 316 (1)
- ✛ Red 347 (1)
- ⋅ Light Red 3328 (1)
- ⊟ Tan 3045 (1)
- ⊕ Yellow 677 (1)
- ▶ Dark Peach 758 (1)
- ⊙ Peach 945 (1)

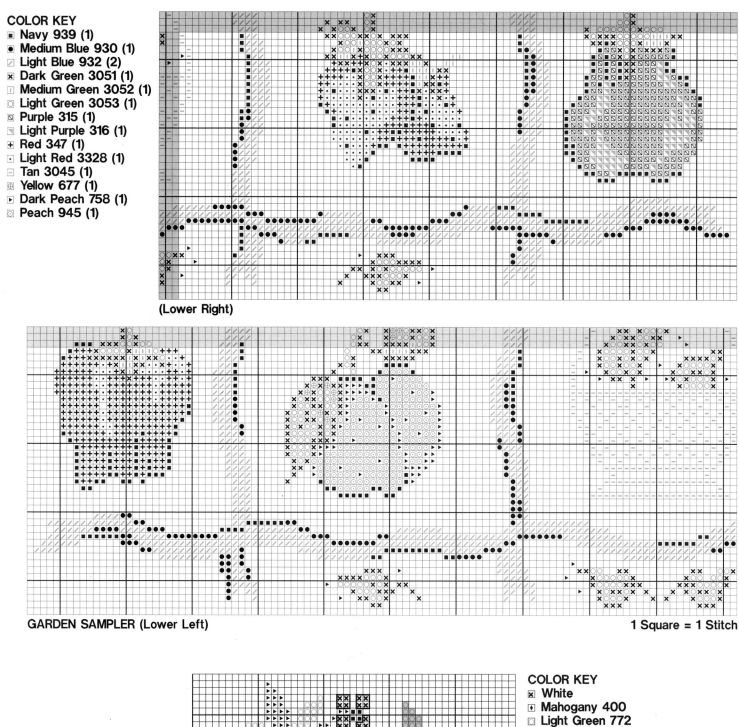

(Lower Right)

GARDEN SAMPLER (Lower Left)

1 Square = 1 Stitch

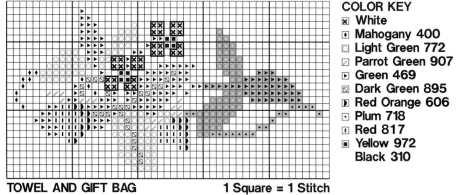

TOWEL AND GIFT BAG **1 Square = 1 Stitch**

COLOR KEY

- ⊠ White
- ◈ Mahogany 400
- ▫ Light Green 772
- ◿ Parrot Green 907
- ▶ Green 469
- ◩ Dark Green 895
- ▯ Red Orange 606
- ⊡ Plum 718
- ⊞ Red 817
- ◼ Yellow 972
- Black 310

136

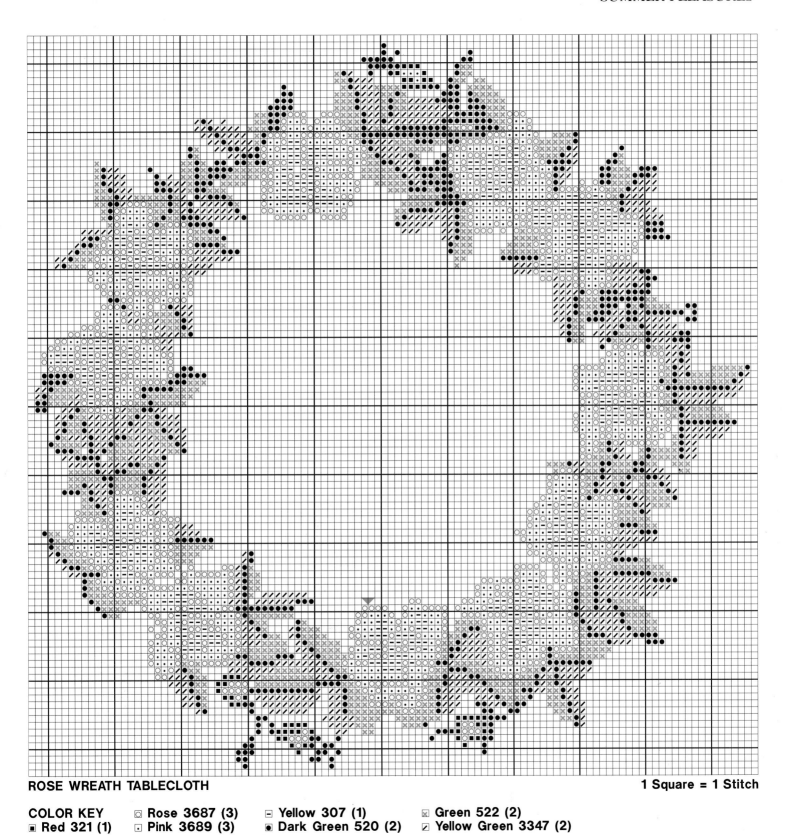

ROSE WREATH TABLECLOTH

1 Square = 1 Stitch

COLOR KEY

⊙ Rose 3687 (3)	⊟ Yellow 307 (1)	⊠ Green 522 (2)
◙ Red 321 (1)	⊡ Pink 3689 (3)	◉ Dark Green 520 (2)	◿ Yellow Green 3347 (2)

Fourth of July–American Country Crafts

Hooray for the Red, White, and Blue, and all of the spectacular designs Old Glory sparks. The star-spangled projects shown here will bring cheers of praise from friends and family at your next Independence Day celebration.

Filled to the brim with hot dogs, potato chips, and cold sliced watermelon, the picnic basket, *left,* will hold almost everything you need for a good old-fashioned Fourth of July get-together. Stitch the design on a field of 18-count Aida cloth; then use it to upholster the lid of a square basket.

The design for the basket is the center portion of the Liberty Sampler, *opposite.* Red and blue borders frame the flags in the center to complete a 20½-inch-square wall hanging, matted and framed as shown.

Patterns for these patriotic projects begin on page 144.

139

Blue-Ribbon Designs–State Fair Pride

Iowa takes great pride in the bounty that nature provides and the Iowa State Fair is one way to display the best of the best. Here, and on the following pages, are blue-ribbon designs that reflect favorite scenes from the fair.

The two youngsters, *right,* dressed in potential award-winning outfits, take a break from fair activities for ice-cream treats. The bibs on their overalls are hardanger fabric cross-stitched with their favorite motifs from the sampler, *opposite.* Lined up in rows, the state fair images fill the sampler, which is a great source for patterns for projects here and on the next two pages. Stitched over two threads of 18-count Aida cloth, the finished wall hanging measures a full 19x31 inches.

Instructions begin on page 146.

Blue-Ribbon Designs–State Fair Pride

Every year Bea brings her pickled cukes to the fair and takes home a blue ribbon. The cross-stitched pickle recipe is a condensed version that she affectionately hangs on her kitchen wall.

Stitched on hardanger fabric, the framed recipe, *far left,* measures 7¾x6¾ inches. The pickle jar border is repeated on the ribbon band and fastened around the filled canning jar. No need to transfer these pickles to another container when serving; the cross-stitched band is a great table decoration.

Red and white pillow ticking and calico fabrics combine with the same pickle jar border to make an apron, *opposite,* that is the envy of every state fair judge. And, wouldn't the pattern be perfect along the edge of kitchen towels or place mats?

Instructions for making these projects are on page 146.

LIBERTY/FREEDOM PICNIC BASKET

Shown on page 138.
Finished size of design is 11x10½ inches.
Design is 99x94 stitches.

MATERIALS
17x17 inches of ecru 18-count Aida cloth
DMC embroidery floss in colors listed on the color key; number of skeins required appears in first set of parentheses
Embroidery hoop
Tapestry needle
Polyester fiberfill
Staple gun
¼-inch plywood cut to cover lid of basket
Carpenter's wood glue

INSTRUCTIONS
Note: The pattern for the picnic basket cover is borrowed from the center of the Liberty/Freedom Sampler chart, *at right.* Work only the central design area, omitting all borders. (See the photograph on page 138.)

The chart for the picnic basket is divided into two sections. Shaded rows on the charts show you where one section overlaps with the next. Do not rework the shaded rows as you move from section to section. These areas are only placement guides.

Hem or tape raw edges of the fabric to prevent threads from raveling as you stitch. Use three strands of floss and work cross-stitches over two threads of fabric.

Measure 5 inches down and 5 inches in from the top left corner of the fabric. Begin working the top point of the upper left star here.

When stitching is complete, press stitchery using a damp cloth and a warm iron.

FINISHING THE BASKET COVER: Cut a piece of polyester fiberfill that is 1 inch larger all the way around than the plywood; lay the fiberfill on top of the plywood. Lay the stitched design, centered, on top of the fiberfill. Turn the stitchery, fiberfill, and plywood upside down, making sure that the fabric and fiberfill do not shift off center.

Pull the fabric and fiberfill taut to the back side of the plywood. Using the staple gun, fasten the fabric to the back side of the plywood.

Glue the covered plywood lid directly on top of the picnic basket lid.

SHORTCUT ASSEMBLY: You may choose to staple the fiberfill and stitchery directly to the basket lid. Trim the stitchery fabric to within 2 inches of the edge of the lid; machine-stitch edge to prevent threads from raveling. Neatly trim and staple the fiberfill and stitchery to the inside of lid, clipping the fiberfill under the stitchery to prevent bulkiness.

LIBERTY/FREEDOM SAMPLER

Shown on page 139.
Finished size of design is 14x14 inches.
Design is 155x155 stitches.

MATERIALS
20x20 inches of ecru hardanger fabric
DMC embroidery floss in colors listed on the color key; number of skeins required appears in the second set of parentheses
Embroidery hoop
Tapestry needle

INSTRUCTIONS
The chart for the sampler shown on page 139 is divided into four sections and printed on pages 144–147. Shaded rows on the charts show you where one section overlaps with the next. Do not rework the shaded rows as you move from section to section. They are only placement guides.

Hem or tape raw edges of the fabric to prevent threads from raveling as you stitch. Use two strands of floss and work cross-stitches over two threads of fabric.

continued

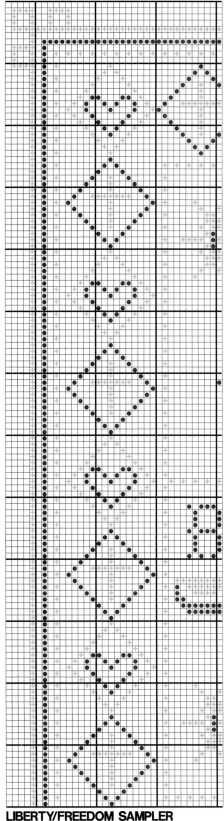

LIBERTY/FREEDOM SAMPLER

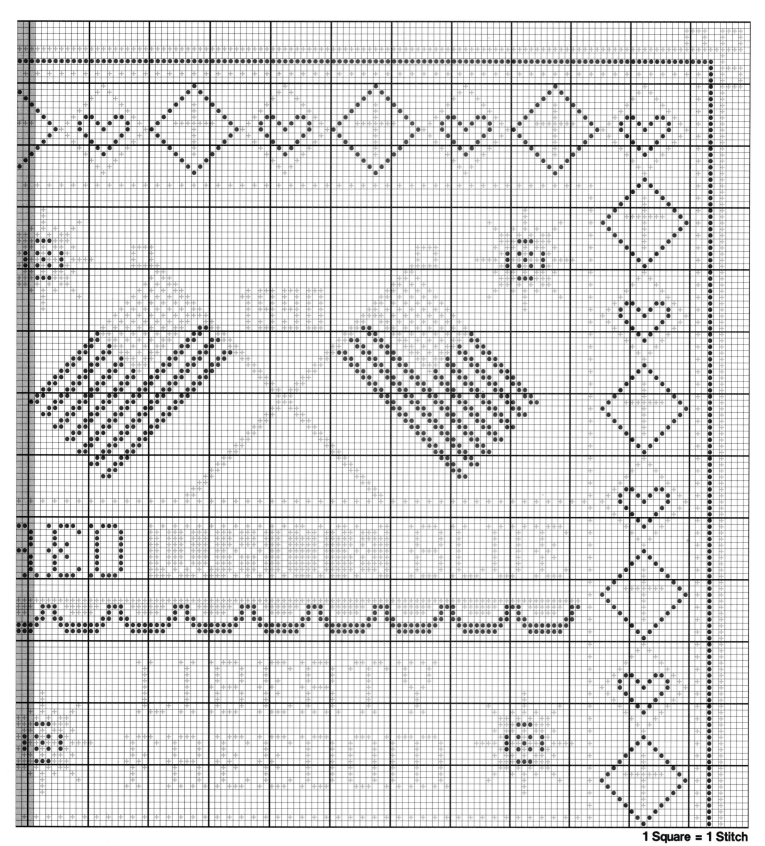

1 Square = 1 Stitch

COLOR KEY ◉ Red (1) (2)   ⊞ Blue (2) (3)

Measure 3 inches down and 3 inches in from the top left corner of the fabric. Begin working the upper left corner of the border here.

When stitching is complete, carefully press the sampler using a damp cloth and a warm iron. Frame stitchery as desired.

BLUE-RIBBON PICKLES APRON

Shown on page 143.
Finished size of design is 10x3 inches.
Design is 110x33 stitches.

MATERIALS
16x16-inch square of ecru hardanger fabric
One skein of DMC embroidery floss in colors listed on the color key
Apron pattern with bib front
Embroidery hoop
Tapestry needle

INSTRUCTIONS
The apron bib design is borrowed from the recipe pattern, *opposite*. Work only the jars, ribbon, and checkerboard motifs. (Refer to the photograph on page 143.) Add or delete pickle jars or checks to fit your own apron bodice pattern.

The apron shown on page 143 is adapted from a pattern from Prairie Patchwork Patterns, 4029 Muskogee, Des Moines, IA 50312. When you assemble the garment, the stitched hardanger takes the place of the front bib fabric.

Hem or tape raw edges of the fabric to prevent threads from raveling as you stitch. Use three strands of floss and work cross-stitches over two threads of fabric.

Measure 8 inches down and 3 inches in from the top left corner of the fabric. Begin working the top left red check here. (See arrows on the chart.)

When stitching is complete, press stitchery using a damp cloth and a warm iron.

Finish according to the instructions included with the pattern.

PICKLE RECIPE

Shown on page 142.
Finished size of design is 5½x3 inches.
Design is 117x67 stitches.

MATERIALS
12x9 inches of ecru hardanger fabric
One skein of DMC embroidery floss in colors listed on the color key
Embroidery hoop
Tapestry needle

INSTRUCTIONS
The pattern for the pickle recipe wall hanging appears *opposite*.

Hem or tape raw edges of the fabric to prevent threads from raveling as you stitch. Use two strands of floss and work cross-stitches over one thread of fabric. Measure 3½ inches down and 3½ inches in from the top left corner of the fabric. Begin working the top left red check here. (See arrows on the chart.)

Backstitch the recipe using two strands of No. 703 light green over one thread of hardanger. Press finished stitchery on back side using a damp cloth and a warm iron; frame as desired.

PICKLE JAR BAND

Shown on page 142.

MATERIALS
Aida cloth ribbon with prefinished edge and 15 threads per inch in a length to fit around jar
One skein of DMC embroidery floss in colors listed on the color key (except bright blue, navy, and gold)
Embroidery hoop
Tapestry needle

INSTRUCTIONS
The ribbon shown in the photograph on page 142 is manufactured by Leisure Arts, Inc., P.O. Box 5595, Little Rock, AR 72215, and is available by the yard through most crafts shops.

LIBERTY/FREEDOM SAMPLER

■ **Red (1) (2)**
⊞ **Blue (2) (3)**

Measure the circumference of the jar that you wish to decorate and purchase a piece of ribbon that length.

Repeat the pickle jar design, *opposite*, omitting the bottom row of checks and the blue ribbon, to fill the length of the ribbon. Begin stitching the bottom left corner check two threads above the bottom edge of the ribbon. Use two strands of floss to work the cross-stitches over one thread of ribbon fabric. Press the back side of the finished stitchery. Place band around jar or container; hand-stitch ends together to hold in place.

STATE FAIR SAMPLER

Shown on page 141.
Finished size of design is 19x31 inches.
Design is 170x281 stitches.

MATERIALS
25x37 inches of 18-count Aida cloth
DMC embroidery floss in colors listed on the color key; number of skeins required appears in parentheses
Embroidery hoop; tapestry needle

INSTRUCTIONS
The chart for the sampler shown on page 141 is divided into sections and printed on pages 148–151.

Shaded areas on the charts show you where one section overlaps with the next.
continued

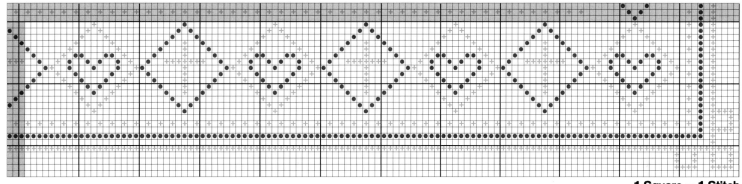

1 Square = 1 Stitch

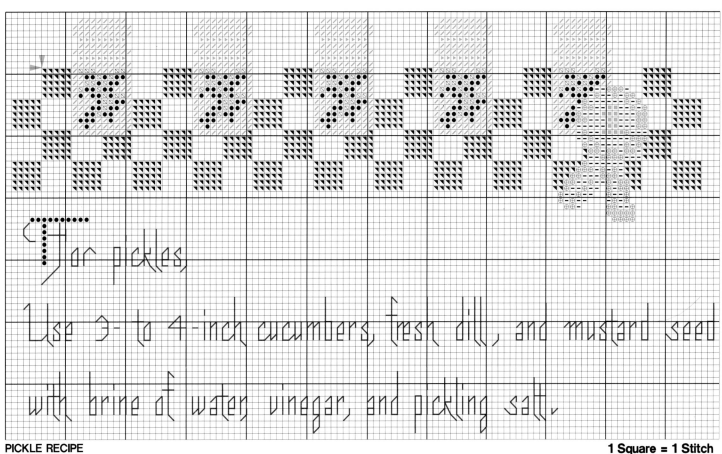

PICKLE RECIPE

1 Square = 1 Stitch

COLOR KEY

◥ Red 817
🔲 Green 937
◉ Light Green 703
▶ Blue 807
⊕ Bright Blue 995
◪ Aqua 993
⊟ Navy 797
▦ Gold 972

FAVORITE DAYS OF SUMMER

Do not rework the shaded rows as you move from section to section. These areas are only placement guides.

Hem or tape raw edges of the fabric to prevent raveling. Use three strands of floss and work cross-stitches over two threads of fabric.

Use two strands to work backstitches over two threads. Backstitch cows and pigs with No. 310 black, and cherry stems and ice cream with No. 801 dark brown. Backstitch the four flagstaffs on the left with No. 310 black and the four on the right with No. 647 gray.

Measure 12 inches down and 3 inches in from the top left corner of the fabric. Begin working the grass under the roller coaster here. The arrow on the chart shows you where to begin. When stitching is complete, press stitchery. Mat and frame as desired.

BOY'S OVERALLS WITH ROLLER COASTER MOTIF

Shown on page 140.
Finished size of design is 7¾x3¾ inches.
Design is 170x82 stitches.

MATERIALS
Ecru hardanger fabric in yardage required for bib front according to pattern
One skein of DMC embroidery floss in colors designated with ** on the color key
Embroidery hoop; tapestry needle
Purchased overalls pattern
Fabric and notions as listed on purchased pattern

INSTRUCTIONS
The roller coaster design from the sampler chart, *right,* is used for the bib on the boy's overalls shown on page 140.

Select a shorts pattern with a bib. (We used Butterick's No. 3748, Size 5.) Substitute hardanger fabric for the bib fabric. Cut out pattern piece for the bib front.

continued

continued

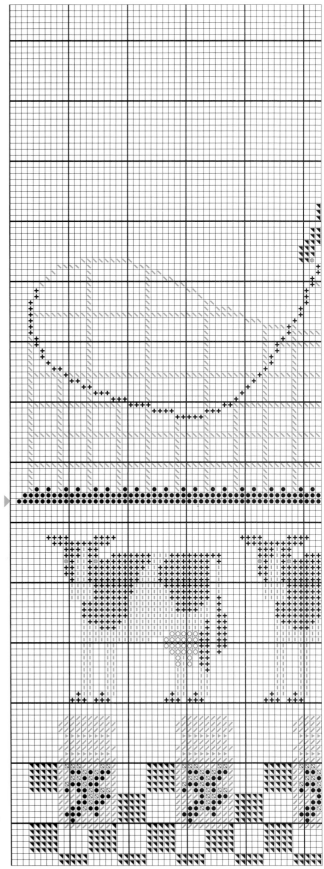

COLOR KEY
☐ **White (2)** ★
◥ **Red 817 (2)** ★ ★★
◎ **Peach 353 (1)**
⊞ **Black 310 (4)** ★★
· **Dark Gray 535 (1)**
◩ **Gray 647 (4)** ★★
▨ **Green 937 (1)**
● **Light Green 703 (3)**★★
▷ **Blue 807 (1)**
⊕ **Bright Blue 995 (2)** ★★
☑ **Aqua 993 (1)**
– **Navy 797 (1)** ★
▦ **Gold 972 (1)** ★★
⊠ **Yellow 973 (1)**
▦ **Rust 301 (1)** ★★
■ **Dark Brown 801 (2)** ★
☐ **Medium Brown 434 (1)** ★
☐ **Light Brown 436 (2)** ★
★ **Used on girl's overalls**
★★ **Used on boy's overalls**

STATE FAIR SAMPLER

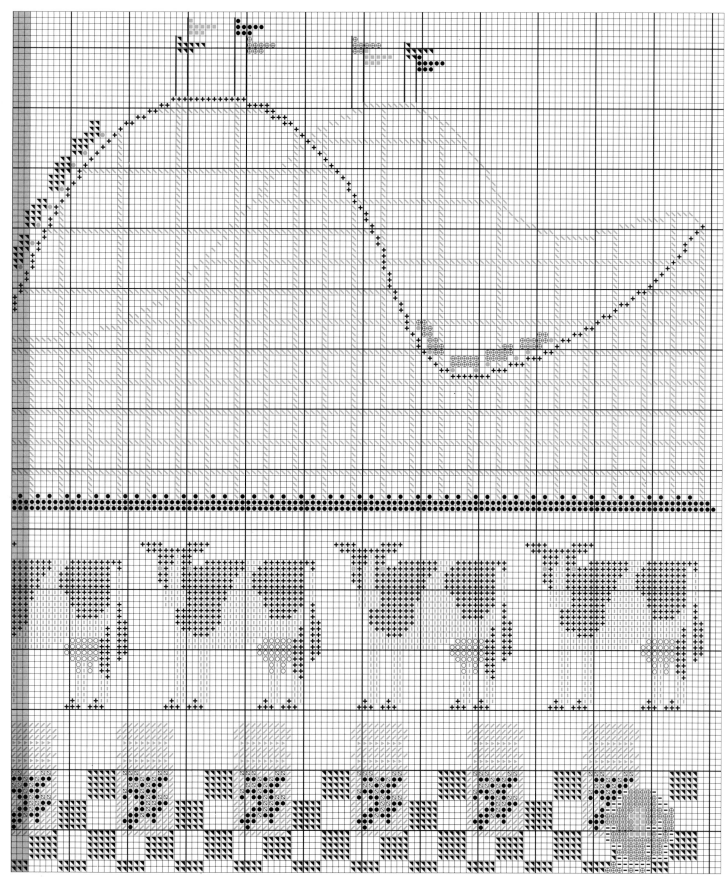

1 Square = 1 Stitch

FAVORITE DAYS OF SUMMER

Draw around piece on hardanger; do not cut out. Center the design horizontally and vertically on the bib front on the hardanger. Use three strands of floss and work cross-stitches over one thread of fabric. Using two strands of floss, backstitch the four flagstaffs on the left with No. 310 black and the four on the right with No. 647 gray. Press stitchery.

Finish following pattern instructions.

GIRL'S OVERALLS WITH ICE-CREAM CONES

Shown on page 140.
Finished size of design is 9¾x3½ inches.
Design is 107x38 stitches.

MATERIALS

Hardanger fabric in yardage required for bib front according to pattern
One skein of DMC embroidery floss in colors designated with * on color key
Embroidery hoop; tapestry needle
Purchased jumper or overalls pattern
Fabric and notions as listed on purchased pattern

INSTRUCTIONS

The ice-cream cones design from the sampler chart, *right,* is used to make the bib on the girl's overalls shown on page 140.

Select an overalls pattern with a bib. (We used a Honey Bunny pattern, No. 5010 from Daisy Kingdom, Portland, OR 97209.) Cross-stitch will be substituted for the fabric on the bib front.

Cut out pattern piece for the bib front. Draw around piece on hardanger; do not cut out. Based on size of overalls pattern and width of bib, determine how many ice-cream cones you need to stitch. Center design horizontally and vertically on the bib front on the hardanger. Use three strands of floss and work cross-stitches over two threads of fabric. Backstitch the cherry stems and around the ice cream with two strands of No. 801 dark brown. Finish according to pattern instructions.

COLOR KEY

☐ White (2) ★
◥ Red 817 (2) ★ ★★
◎ Peach 353 (1)
⊞ Black 310 (4) ★★
⊡ Dark Gray 535 (1)
◪ Gray 647 (4) ★★
◩ Green 937 (1)
◉ Light Green 703 (3) ★★
▷ Blue 807 (1)
⊕ Bright Blue 995 (2) ★★
☑ Aqua 993 (1)
⊟ Navy 797 (1) ★
▣ Gold 972 (1) ★★
☒ Yellow 973 (1)
▨ Rust 301 (1) ★★
◼ Dark Brown 801 (2) ★
▢ Medium Brown 434 (1) ★
▣ Light Brown 436 (2) ★
★ Used on girl's overalls
★★ Used on boy's overalls

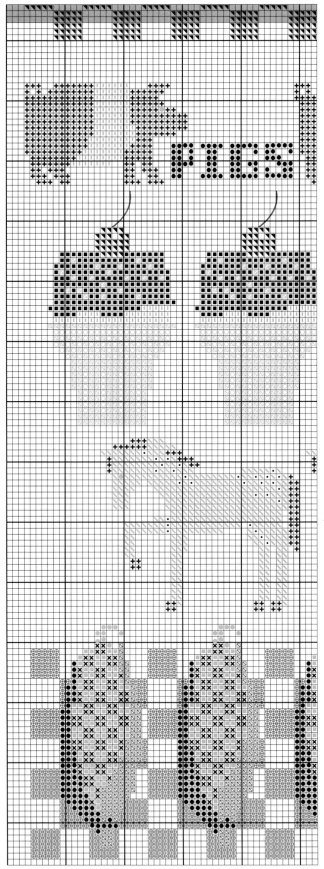

STATE FAIR SAMPLER

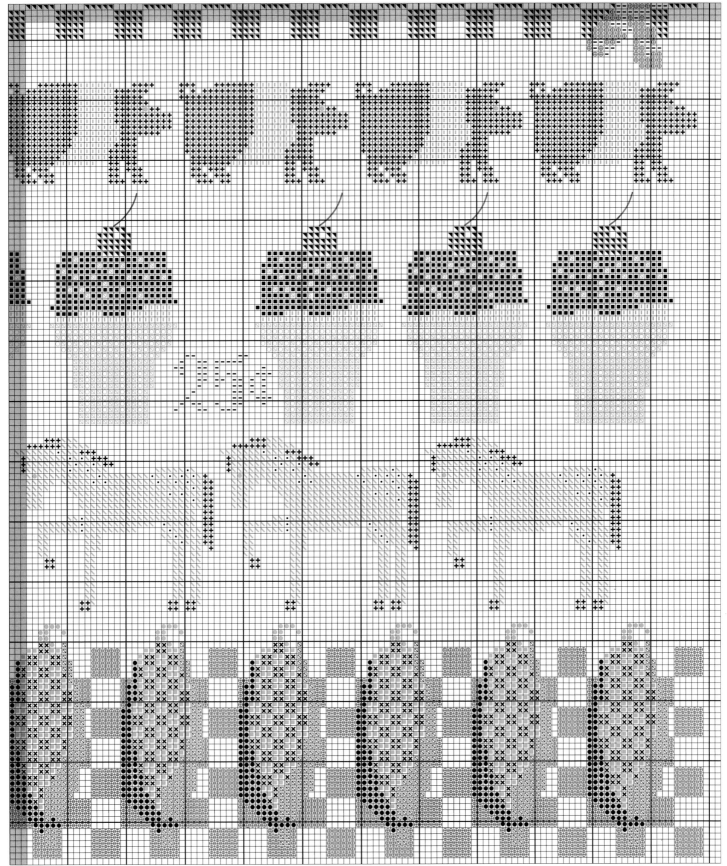

1 Square = 1 Stitch

Precious Gifts to Welcome Baby

Creating a cross-stitched wall hanging that records the birth of a new baby is a loving gesture. Sampler stitching is a great tradition and this memento will become one of this child's treasured keepsakes.

To announce the birth of a special baby, make the colorful pillow, *right.* Stitched on 16-count Aida cloth, the design uses bright colors and imitates Pennsylvania Dutch folk art.

The sampler, *opposite,* uses borders and hearts to full advantage in proclaiming baby's arrival. A checkerboard edging frames the names and date on the 13¼ x 15¼-inch framed wall hanging.

With a few simple changes in the written messages on both pieces, the patterns can be used for any occasion.

Instructions for these projects are on pages 156 and 159.

152

Sarah
Elizabeth

MARCH 1, 1990

21 inches 7 lbs. 4 oz.

SUE and DAVID
ANDERSON

Gifts for Baby's Nap and Snack Times

Besides the enjoyment of cross-stitching, it's the little extras that make baby gifts fun to create. These patterns will inspire a variety of gifts for children.

The soft, stuffed "baby sleeping" door sign, *above*, combines two techniques—backstitching and painting. Use the backstitches to outline the design, then brush acrylic paint in pale pastels onto hair, skin, and clothing. Finish with satin ribbon roses.

The "chew chew" train on the terry-cloth bib, *opposite*, makes preparing for snack time more appealing to any child. This practical cover-up has snaps at the neck and under the arms, and covers most of a child's clothing.

Instructions begin on page 159.

BIRTH SAMPLER

Shown on page 153.
Finished size of design is 9x11 inches.
Design is 99x123 stitches.

MATERIALS

15x17-inch piece of white 22-count
  even-weave fabric (hardanger)
DMC embroidery floss in colors listed
  on the color key; number of skeins
  required appears in parentheses
Embroidery hoop; tapestry needle
Graph paper

INSTRUCTIONS

The chart for the sampler is located on
page 157.

Chart names of the baby and parents,
and the baby's length, weight, and date of
birth on a sheet of graph paper using the
alphabets and numbers provided at *right*.
(Refer to the chart, *opposite,* and the photograph on page 153 to identify which alphabet to use for each portion of the
sampler.)

Hem or tape the raw edges of the fabric
to prevent threads from raveling as you
work. Use three strands and work cross-
stitches over two threads of fabric. Work
French knots over one thread.

Measure 3 inches from the left side of
the fabric and 3 inches from the top; begin
stitching the upper left corner of the sampler here.

Stitch the checkerboard pattern first,
then the garland with hearts and bows. Fill
in the center of the sampler last.

Refer to the photograph or chart for
placement of names and dates. Center
each line on the sampler. Using two
strands of floss, backstitch the date,
weight, and length of the baby. Use
French knots for periods after the length
and weight abbreviations.

Use No. 554 lavender for the parents'
and baby's names; No. 742 gold for the
birth date; and No. 807 light blue for the
length and weight of the baby.

When the sampler is finished, remove
the tape and press carefully on the wrong
side using a damp cloth and warm iron.
Frame as desired.

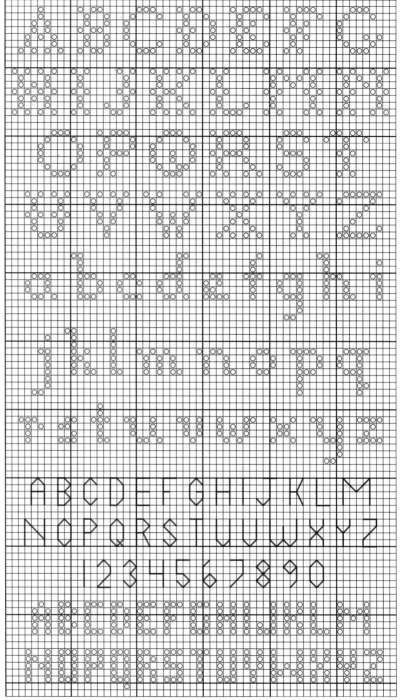

BIRTH SAMPLER   **1 Square = 1 Stitch**

COLOR KEY
▨ Pink 899 (1)
⊞ Light Pink 3326 (2)
▷ Rose 326 (1)
▨ Gold 742 (1)

▨ Blue 517 (1)
▨ Light Blue 807 (1)
▨ Turquoise 943 (1)
◎ Lavender 554 (1)

BIRTH SAMPLER

MARCH 1, 1987

21 in.   7 lbs. 4 oz.

1 Square = 1 Stitch

BIRTH ANNOUNCEMENT PILLOW

1 Square = 1 Stitch

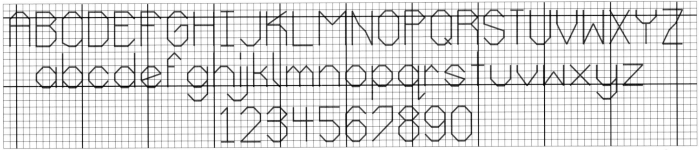

BIRTH ANNOUNCEMENT PILLOW

1 Square = 1 Stitch

COLOR KEY
- ◙ Magenta 917
- ◩ Purple Blue 792
- ◉ Gold 680
- ◪ Yellow 725
- ⊠ Medium Green 904
- ▶ Yellow Green 704
- ⊞ Green Blue 958
- Dark Green 890

BIRTH ANNOUNCEMENT PILLOW

Shown on page 152.
Finished size of design is 6x7¼ inches.
Design is 101x116 stitches.

MATERIALS
12x13-inch piece of ecru 16-count Aida cloth
One skein of DMC embroidery floss in colors listed on the color key
Embroidery hoop
Graph paper
Needle

INSTRUCTIONS
The chart for the pillow appears *opposite*.

Chart the birth date and the baby's and parents' names on a sheet of graph paper using the letters and numbers provided *above*. (Refer to the photograph on page 152 and the chart for guidance.)

Hem or tape the raw edges of the fabric to prevent threads from raveling as you work. Use three strands of floss for cross-stitches and two strands for backstitches. Work each cross-stitch and backstitch over one thread of the fabric.

Complete cross-stitches first, then back-stitch the date and names according to the chart and your own graph.

Use No. 890 dark green for the general lettering shown on the chart; use No. 917 magenta for the specific date and names.

Measure 6 inches in and 3 inches down from the top left of the fabric; begin stitching here. (The arrows on the pattern show you where to begin.)

When stitching is complete, remove the tape. Press the stitchery carefully on the wrong side using a damp cloth and warm iron.

Finish pillow as desired.

BABY SLEEPING DOOR SIGN

Shown on page 154.
Finished size is 9x5¼ inches.

MATERIALS
9x13-inch piece of hardanger fabric
One skein of DMC floss in No. 801 brown
Tracing paper
Tapestry needle
Embroidery hoop
⅓ yard of fabric for backing and cording cover
1 yard of cording
Acrylic paint in blue, beige, and rose
Stencil brush
2 yards of satin ribbon
2 purchased ribbon roses
Polyester fiberfill

INSTRUCTIONS
Refer to the chart on the top of page 160. Using the tracing paper, transfer the outline of the entire design to the hardanger, centering the design horizontally and vertically.

Work the entire design in backstitches using three strands of brown floss over two threads of hardanger.

When all stitching is complete, press the fabric carefully on the back side.

Dipping the stencil brush in the paint, lightly brush shadows of color in areas shaded on the pattern as follows: Use blue on the booties, rose on the shirt, and beige on the arms and legs. *Note:* Before shading, be sure to tap the brush on a paper towel to get rid of excess paint. The brush should have little paint on the ends of the bristles when you add the shading. Practice on scrap fabric before you add the color to the finished stitchery.

Finish pillow as desired. Add satin ribbon hanger with ribbon roses and green satin bows at each upper corner. Refer to the photograph on page 154.

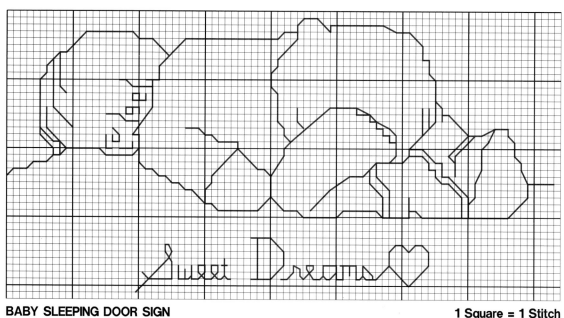

BABY SLEEPING DOOR SIGN

1 Square = 1 Stitch

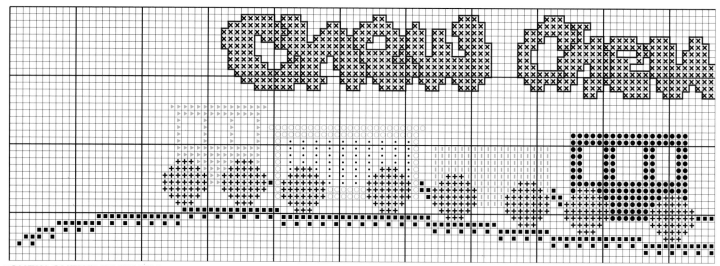

"CHEW CHEW" BABY BIB

"CHEW CHEW" BABY BIB

Shown on page 155.
Finished size of bib including ruffle is 14x18 inches.
Design is 35x177 stitches.

MATERIALS

One 7x18-inch strip each of white 14-count Aida cloth and lightweight interfacing
One skein of DMC embroidery floss in colors listed on the color key
Tracing paper
Embroidery hoop
Tapestry needle
¾ yard of red terry cloth
½ yard of 1½-inch-wide red ribbing
¾ yard of wide double-fold bias tape
2½ yards of a 1-inch-wide white pregathered eyelet ruffle
2½ yards of a 1¾-inch-wide pregathered red calico ruffle
Two decorative snaps (back closures)
Two regular snaps (side closures)

INSTRUCTIONS

The chart for the bib is given in two sections, *opposite* and *below*. Work the left side of the pattern first, then the right side. *Note:* The shaded rows of stitches on the right side are repeated from the left side and are used only as a guide in moving from one pattern section to the other. Do not rework these rows of stitches.

Hem or tape raw edges of fabric to prevent threads from raveling as you work. Use two strands of floss and work cross-stitches and backstitches over one thread of fabric.

Measure 3 inches up and 3 inches in from the bottom left corner of the cloth. Begin stitching the left end of the train track there.

After all cross-stitching is completed, backstitch around the smoke (lettering) using No. 796 blue; take two backstitches on the cowcatcher (the front of the train) using No. 310 black.

Press finished stitchery on back side.

ASSEMBLY: Trim stitched fabric 1 inch beyond last row of stitches at top and bottom of design. Trim fabric 1½ inches beyond the last row of stitches on both the left and right sides. Fabric strip will measure 4½x15¾ inches.

Cut interfacing to measure 4½x15¾ inches. Right sides facing, sew interfacing to stitched fabric along top and bottom edges. Turn right side out; press with damp cloth and warm iron. Set aside.

Trace a 15½x25½-inch rectangle onto terry cloth; baste on this line, then cut out just beyond stitching.

Fold rectangle in half crosswise to make a 15½x12¾-inch rectangle. Measure in 5 inches on each side of one 12¾-inch side. From those points, measure down 1 inch on each side. Measure down 1½ inches from center top. Using these points as a guideline, cut out an oval through both thicknesses to form the neckline. Cut center back seam open from neckline edge to bottom of bib.

Sew ribbing to neckline using a ¼-inch seam. Clip into the terry-cloth seam allowance. Topstitch around neck edge close to the seam, through bib and seam allowance. Bind center back edges with bias tape. Attach snap fasteners to bib back.

Topstitch cross-stitched fabric to bib front 2¼ inches from bottom edge. Trim excess fabric on sides.

Sew eyelet and calico ruffles around outside edge of bib using ¼-inch seam. Press seam to wrong side; topstitch close to ruffling seam through all thicknesses.

Center and sew a snap on each side of the bib to fasten under baby's arms.

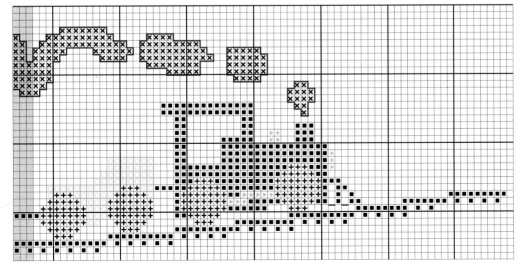

1 Square = 1 Stitch

COLOR KEY
☐ Orange 608
⊡ Yellow 445
▷ Red 666
⦿ Blue 796
⊠ Light Blue 809
☐ Green 909
⊞ Gray 415
▣ Black 310

Nature's Vibrant Colors
AUTUMN'S SPLENDOR

The sunlight of autumn brings out the intense colors of the season. The crunch of oak and maple leaves underfoot and a gentle nip in the air make fall many people's favorite time of year.

The detailed filigree designs on the pillows, *left,* show the richness of cross-stitching in a monochromatic, or one-color, scheme. Borrowed from filet-crocheted patterns, these motifs are worked on even-weave fabric with 18 squares to the inch. Complete the 15-inch-square pillows with piping and ruffles in coordinating colors.

Instructions begin on page 169.

As fall approaches, Mother Nature paints the countryside with a palette of rich rusts, browns, oranges, and reds. The vibrant pheasant is a natural autumn design element for cross-stitchers.

The single male pheasant, *left,* is a handsome choice for the jewelry box insert. The warm jewel tones of the embroidery floss complement the walnut finish of the box. Work the 7x5-inch insert on 30-count linen fabric.

A pheasant border turns a simple wool stadium blanket into a handsome throw, *opposite,* for a man's den. Stitch the repeat pattern on a linen fabric that has approximately 30 threads to the inch; then, machine-stitch the border to the blanket of your choice.

Patterns and instructions for these projects begin on page 170.

ABC's of Country
apples 🍎 baskets of berries 🌹
clusters of cherries 🍒 daisies
in the meadow ⚓ eggs over easy
family reunions ✕✕✕✕✕ gaggles
of geese ♥ hearts 🌷 I love you
jam and jelly ✕ kitchen cupboard
🌸 lilac bushes ❋ making bread 🌸
nosegays ✕ open windows ✕ picnic
baskets 🌷 quilts ⚓ rocking chair
singing in the rain 🐦 taffy pull
utterly delicious blueberry pie
valentines ✕ wildflower wreaths
⭕ xtra special moments 🐦
yuletide ribbons 🐝 z-z-z-z-z-z-z

Baskets of pumpkins, bowls of colorful gourds, and shocks of cornstalks standing in the fields—harvesttime makes autumn a memorable season.

A wall hanging of the "ABC's of Country," *opposite*, reflects activities and sights that make the rural life so appealing. Colorful hearts and flowers punctuate thoughts in this 20½x27½-inch framed stitchery worked with three strands of floss on Aida cloth.

A red barn with a silo is the main focus for the farm blessing, *above*. Cross-stitched on ecru hardanger, the wall hanging has a charming border of farm men and women surrounding a wish for abundant crops at harvesttime.

Instructions are on page 175.

AUTUMN PILLOWS

COLOR KEY
◻ **Teal 991 (11)**

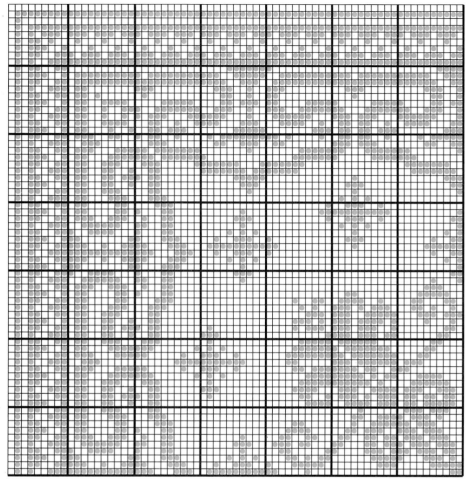

1 Square = 1 Stitch

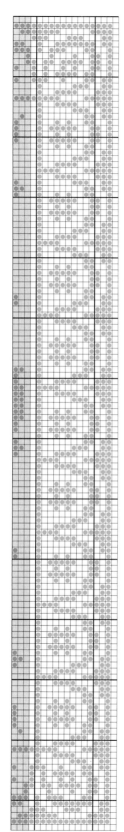

COLOR KEY
◻ **Salmon 347 (11)**

1 Square = 1 Stitch

AUTUMN PILLOWS

Shown on pages 162 and 163.
Finished size of each design is 15 inches
square or 135 stitches square.

MATERIALS
For one pillow
22-inch square of even-weave fabric with
 18 threads per inch
11 skeins of DMC embroidery floss in
 No. 347 salmon or No. 991 teal
1½ yards of fabric for backing, piping,
 and ruffle
2 yards of cording
Polyester fiberfill
Embroidery hoop; tapestry needle

INSTRUCTIONS
The chart, *left,* is for the pillow shown in
salmon on pages 162 and 163.

 The chart, *above,* is for the teal pillow
shown in the photo on pages 162–163.
The pattern, *above,* represents one-fourth
of the design and is for the upper left-
hand quarter. For ease in working, you
may want to chart the complete design
onto graph paper before beginning to
stitch.

 The outside row on the two sides join-
ing quadrants represents the center of
each side. These rows should be stitched
only one time.

 Tape raw edges of fabric to prevent
fraying. Use three strands of floss to work
cross-stitches over two threads of fabric.
continued

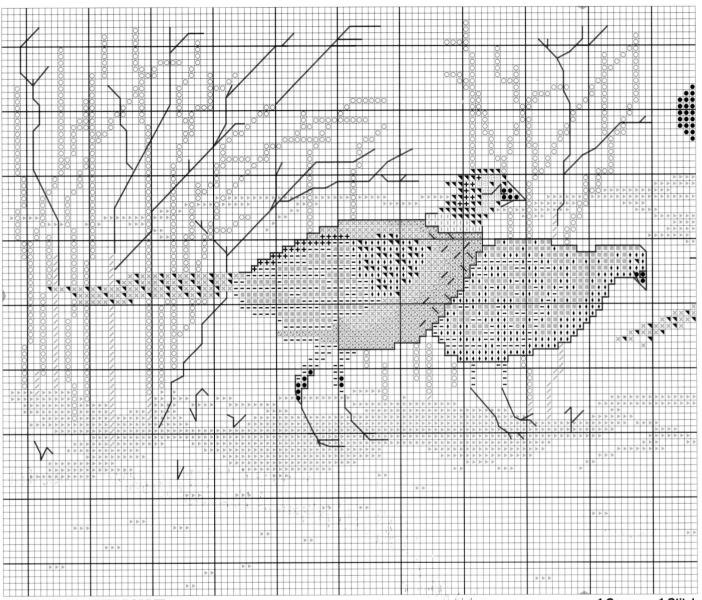

PHEASANT BLANKET BORDER

1 Square = 1 Stitch

COLOR KEY

⊡	White (1)	⊟	Dark Brown 801 (1)
⦿	Yellow 744 (1)	⊠	Brown 301 (1)
⊙	Gold 834 (3)	⬧	Light Brown 435 (1)
⬚	Avocado 830 (1)	◤	Black Brown 3371 (1)
▷	Gray 3024 (4)	▦	Tan 437 (1)
⊠	Rust 922 (2)	⊞	Red 347 (1)
		✚	Teal 992 (1)

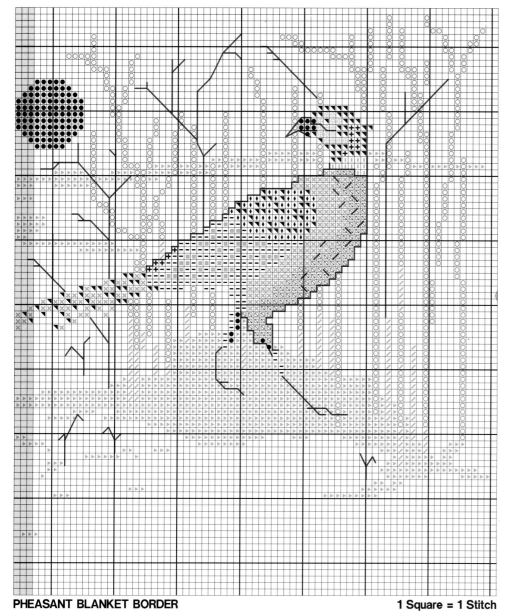

PHEASANT BLANKET BORDER

1 Square = 1 Stitch

Measure 3 inches down and 3 inches in from the top left corner; begin stitching upper left corner here. When stitching is complete, remove tape. Press stitchery on the back side. Finish as desired.

PHEASANTS BLANKET AND JEWELRY BOX

Shown on pages 164 and 165.
Each repeat of three pheasants is 11½ inches long. Finished box insert is 7x5 inches.

MATERIALS
For blanket border
Two 10x70-inch strips of taupe even-weave fabric with 30 threads per inch (We used 70-inch-wide Amaretto Murano fabric from Wichelt Imports)
DMC embroidery floss in colors listed on the color key; number of skeins required appears in parentheses
Tapestry needle; embroidery hoop
Purchased blanket
Contrasting fabric and cord for piping

For jewelry box
11x9 inches of even-weave fabric with 30 threads per inch
One skein each of DMC embroidery floss in colors listed on the color key
Tapestry needle; embroidery hoop
Box with 7x5-inch needlework insert

INSTRUCTIONS
For blanket border
Border pattern is at *left*. Shaded rows on page 171 are repeated from page 170 and should be used only as a guide in moving from one section to the other. Do not re-work these stitches.

Cut a strip of even-weave fabric the width of the blanket plus two inches on each side. Baste a centerline along the
continued

length of the strip. Using this as a reference point, stitch the pheasant motifs. Center the first motif in the center of the fabric strip. An arrow on the chart marks the center row of stitches. No space is left between repeats.

Use two strands of floss and work the cross-stitches over two threads of fabric.

Use two strands of No. 830 avocado for long stitches in foliage, and No. 834 gold for long stitches in snow. Using one strand of floss, backstitch the outline of the pheasants' bodies with No. 801 dark brown, and of the beaks, feet, and markings on breasts with No. 3371 black-brown.

Press the stitchery on the back side.

ASSEMBLY: Trim the even-weave fabric 1½ inches past the stitchery along the top and bottom; this includes ½-inch seam allowances. Mark the length to fit the finished width of the blanket.

Cover cord with fabric to make piping for top and bottom of the stitchery. Cut backing strip to same size as stitchery. Fold under one long edge of backing ½ inch; press. Stitch piping to front of stitchery along seam lines. With right sides of stitchery and blanket facing, stitch together along piping line. Fold and press.

With right sides facing, stitch backing to stitchery along top seam line. Sew short ends of stitchery and backing closed. Trim seams; clip corners. Turn edging; blind-stitch folded edge of backing to blanket.

For the box
The jewelry box shown on page 164 is from Sudberry House, Colton Road, Old Lyme, Conn., and is available in most crafts shops.

The insert chart is *below*.

Hem or tape raw edges of fabric to prevent threads from raveling as you work.

Measure down 2 inches and in 2 inches from the upper left corner of the fabric. Begin stitching the upper left corner of the design here. (See arrows on chart.) Work all cross-stitches using two strands of floss over two threads of fabric.

Press the finished stitchery on the back side. Mount the stitchery in the box top following the manufacturer's instructions.

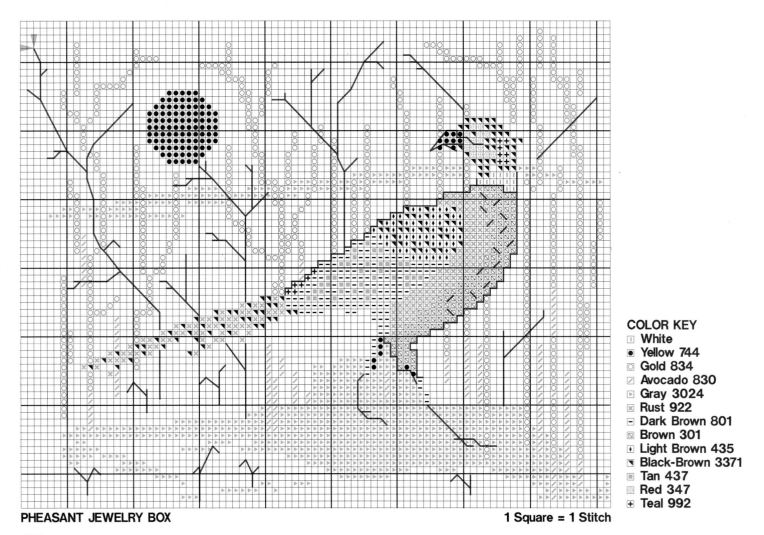

COLOR KEY
- ⊡ White
- ⊙ Yellow 744
- ◎ Gold 834
- ⊘ Avocado 830
- ▷ Gray 3024
- ⊠ Rust 922
- ⊟ Dark Brown 801
- ⊠ Brown 301
- ⊞ Light Brown 435
- ◥ Black-Brown 3371
- ▦ Tan 437
- ⊞ Red 347
- ⊞ Teal 992

PHEASANT JEWELRY BOX   1 Square = 1 Stitch

BLESS THIS FARM WALL HANGING

1 Square = 1 Stitch

COLOR KEY

▶ Ecru	⊠ Brick 221	☑ Dark Blue 797
◉ Red 666	▷ Salmon 3328	⊟ Blue 932
◉ Rose 309	✚ Rust 301	⊠ Dark Aqua 991
⊟ Light Rose 899	⊡ Black Brown 3371	◪ Aqua 992
	⊟ Gray 414	▥ Turquoise 598

⊟ Plum 915	⊞ Dark Green 909
◫ Flesh 945	⊙ Green 905
◥ Gold 832	⊠ Light Green 907
⊞ Yellow 743	
◻ Pistachio 367	

A Bushel of Country

apples • baskets of berries •
clusters of cherries • daisies
in the meadow • eggs over easy
family reunions • gaggles
of geese • hearts • I love you
jam and jelly • kitchen cupboard
• lilac bushes • making bread •
nosegays • open windows • picnic
baskets • quilts • rocking chair
singing in the rain • taffy pull
utterly delicious blueberry pie

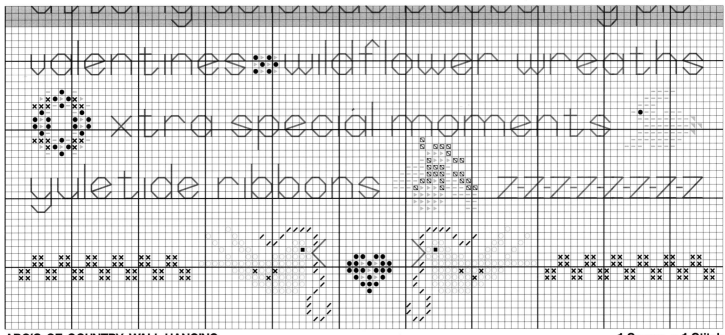

ABC'S OF COUNTRY WALL HANGING

1 Square = 1 Stitch

COLOR KEY
- ⊙ **Red 349 (2)**
- ▷ **Orange 971 (1)**
- ◼ **Dark Blue 791 (2)**
- ⊠ **Blue 322 (1)**
- ☐ **Light Blue 794 (1)**
- ☑ **Green 904 (1)**
- ◹ **Dark Brown 3021 (1)**
- ⊟ **Gray 646 (1)**
- ⊠ **Black 310 (1)**

"BLESS THIS FARM" WALL HANGING

Shown on page 167.
Finished size of design is 8x9¼ inches.
Design is 92x104 stitches.

MATERIALS
12x13-inch piece of ecru hardanger
One skein each of DMC embroidery
  floss in colors listed on the color key
Tapestry needle; embroidery hoop

INSTRUCTIONS
Hem or tape raw edges of fabric to prevent threads from raveling as you work. Refer to the chart on page 173 for stitching. Use three strands of floss and work cross-stitches and backstitches over two threads of fabric. All backstitching is shown by red lines on the pattern and is worked with No. 3371 black-brown.

Measure 2 inches down and 2 inches in from the top left corner of the cloth. Begin stitching the upper left corner of the border there.

When stitching is complete, remove tape; press stitchery on wrong side, using a damp cloth and warm iron. Frame as desired.

"ABC'S OF COUNTRY" WALL HANGING

Shown on page 166.
Finished size is 20½x27½ inches framed.
Design is 106x157 stitches.

MATERIALS
24x31-inch piece of ecru 14-count Aida
  cloth
DMC embroidery floss in colors listed
  on the color key; number of skeins
  required appears in parentheses
Embroidery hoop; tapestry needle

INSTRUCTIONS
Hem or tape raw edges of fabric to prevent threads from raveling as you work. Refer to the chart, *opposite* and *above.* Note: Shaded stitches *above* are repeated from page 174 and should be used only as a guide in moving from one page to the other. Do not rework these stitches.

Measure 3 inches down and 3 inches in from top left corner of the cloth. Begin stitching the top point of letter A here.

Use three strands of floss and work all cross-stitches and backstitches over two threads of fabric.

Use two strands of floss to backstitch the robin's beak with No. 3021 dark brown, and the bluebirds' beaks and all lettering with No. 791 dark blue. When stitchery is finished, remove tape; press using a damp cloth and a warm iron. Frame as desired.

175

Back to School For Kids and Teachers

Kids can have only so much summer fun! Then, it's time to get out the lunch box and books, and head back to the classroom. But a special teacher can turn those school days into happy memories.

You'll be the apple of the teacher's eye if you make the A-plus stitchery, *left,* to show your appreciation. Worked on 14-count Aida cloth, the message is backstitched on a cross-stitched blackboard, complete with chalk and eraser. The pattern on page 185 includes an alphabet for adding your own teacher's name.

The little red schoolhouse takes on a new look in the sampler, *opposite.* From the bell in the steeple to the bright red apples and the students busy at their desks, the elements quickly remind us of grade school. An open doorway is the right size for both the teacher's and student's names and the date of the gift.

Instructions for both projects are on page 187.

Back to School For Kids and Teachers

Inexpensive sweatshirts are transformed into one-of-a-kind cover-ups when you add a band of even-weave cloth stitched with the motifs featured here.

Ecru hardanger, worked with brightly colored embroidery floss, is applied to purchased sweatshirts, *opposite.* Strips of fabric-covered cording can be used to pipe the stitchery to coordinate with a skirt or turtleneck.

The close-ups, *above,* show you the detail in the dinosaurs and the falling stars.

Use your imagination to adapt these designs to all kinds of kids' clothing and room accessories.

Both projects are stitched with three strands of floss over two threads of fabric. Backstitching outlines the girls, stars, dinosaurs, and balloons.

Instructions begin on page 184.

178

Frightfully Simple Crafts For Halloween

Boys and "ghouls" will delight in this not-so-wicked cast of Halloween accessories that can be stitched almost as fast as you can say "boo."

Kids can decorate their own funny-face Halloween treats by using purchased sugar cookies, a can of icing, food coloring, and a variety of candies. Challenge them to see who can make the best face, and watch the fun they have.

The canvas bag with the mischievous trio from the pumpkin patch is a large 15x14 inches. It's sure to hold lots of goodies as trick-or-treaters go from door to door. The cross-stitch is worked on 14-count Aida cloth, which is then stitched onto the fabric-lined bag.

Purchased sweatshirts and waste canvas with 8½ squares to the inch make the Halloween tops, *opposite,* quick and easy to assemble. Add as many spiders, ants, and bats as you dare.

Instructions for all these projects begin on page 187.

Giving Thanks For the Year's Blessings

A bountiful table for your Thanksgiving celebration will be especially elegant when set with the linens shown here. Rich colors mock the changing leaves of the autumn countryside.

One or two stems of wheat are a simple and graceful motif for place mats and napkins, *above.* The head of wheat is worked in cross-stitches and long stitches with two strands of embroidery floss.

Wheat and leaves combine to form the stunning fall wreath on the tablecloth, *op-posite.* The pattern is repeated four times to complete the design. An even-weave fabric with 25 threads per inch makes these table linens look exquisite.

Instructions for these projects begin on page 189.

182

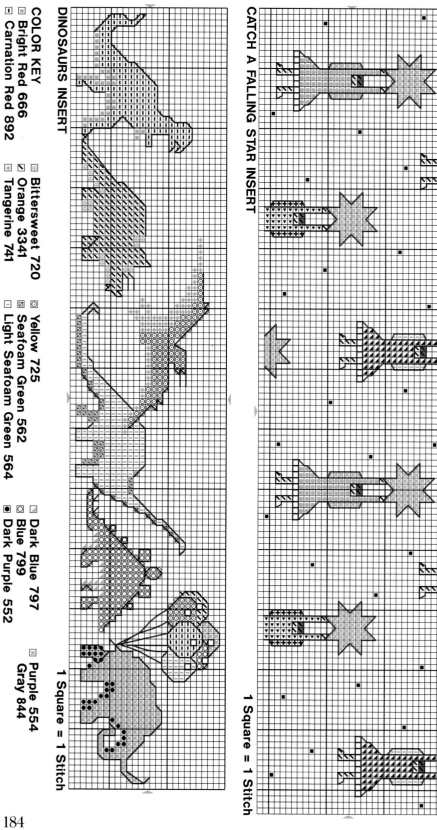

DINOSAURS INSERT

CATCH A FALLING STAR INSERT

COLOR KEY

⊡	Carnation Red 892
⊞	Bright Red 666
⊡	Bittersweet 720
⊠	Yellow 725
⊻	Orange 3341
◨	Seafoam Green 562
⊕	Tangerine 741
⊟	Light Seafoam Green 564

⊘	Dark Blue 797
⊙	Blue 799
◉	Dark Purple 552
⊠	Purple 554
	Gray 844

1 Square = 1 Stitch

1 Square = 1 Stitch

SWEATSHIRT INSERTS

Shown on pages 178 and 179.
Dinosaur design is 128x25 stitches; falling
star design is 132x30 stitches.

MATERIALS
For one shirt
Purchased sweatshirt
16x6 inches of ecru hardanger
One skein of DMC embroidery floss in
   colors listed on the color key
Tapestry needle
Embroidery hoop
Fabric-covered cording (optional)

INSTRUCTIONS
Charts for the designs appear at *left.* The
entire design for each shirt is worked on
hardanger, then stitchery is sewn on the
sweatshirt. Piping is optional.
   Hem or tape raw edges of fabric to prevent threads from raveling as you work.

For the dinosaurs
   Locate the center of the pattern and the
center of the strip of fabric. Arrows on the
chart mark the vertical and horizontal centers. Begin stitching here.
   Use three strands of floss and work
cross-stitches over two threads of fabric.
Use two strands of floss and work backstitches over two threads of fabric.
   Backstitch the dinosaurs and balloons
as follows: the red ones with No. 666
bright red; the yellow ones with No. 741
tangerine; the orange ones with No. 720
bittersweet; the green ones with No. 562
seafoam green; the blue ones with No.
797 dark blue; and the purple ones with
No. 552 dark purple. Backstitch balloon
strings with No. 844 gray.

COLOR KEY

◼	Gold 972
⊠	Yellow 744
◨	Aqua 964
⊠	Peach 754
⊞	Rust 301
⊠	Rose 604
◻	Brown 436
▽	Blue 794
⊡	Dark Aqua 958
▲	Dark Blue 792
◢	Dark Rust 300
	Dark Rose 601
	Dark Brown 434

For the falling stars

Locate the center of the pattern and the center of the strip of fabric. Arrows on the chart mark the vertical and horizontal centers. Begin stitching here.

Use three strands of floss and work cross-stitches over two threads of fabric. Use two strands of floss and work backstitches over two threads of fabric.

A symbol that is shaded pink designates that a French knot will be worked over the cross-stitch when all cross-stitching is finished. Make French knots for eyes using one strand of No. 792 dark blue floss.

Backstitch the pink dresses with No. 601 dark rose, the aqua dresses with No. 958 dark aqua, and the blue dresses with No. 792 dark blue. Backstitch the outline of the stars with No. 972 gold. Backstitch the hands, faces, and legs with No. 300 dark rust. Backstitch the rust hair with No. 300 dark rust; the brown hair with No. 434 dark brown; and the yellow hair with No. 972 gold.

TO FINISH SWEATSHIRTS: Remove tape from stitchery; press stitchery on back side.

Fold top and bottom of stitched hardanger to back side approximately ½ inch from design; press again.

Machine-stitch piping to top and bottom edges of fabric strip along fold.

Remove threads of sweatshirt to open sleeve and side seams along front beginning approximately 3½ inches down from neckline. Make an opening 5 inches long.

Position stitched strip of fabric 3½ inches below neckline, centering design across front of sweatshirt. Insert ends into sleeve seam openings. Machine-topstitch along top and bottom of stitchery, sewing in the ditch atop the piping seam.

Turn sweatshirt inside out. With right sides facing, restitch sleeve and side seams. Turn sweatshirt right side out; press again, if desired.

A+ TEACHER   **1 Square = 1 Stitch**

COLOR KEY
- ⊡ White
- ▶ Red 321
- ◤ Pink 962
- ▢ Green 469
- ▨ Light Green 907
- ⊞ Tan 422
- ▨ Brown Gray 3021
- ⊠ Light Gray 415
- ▢ Aqua 993
- Black 310

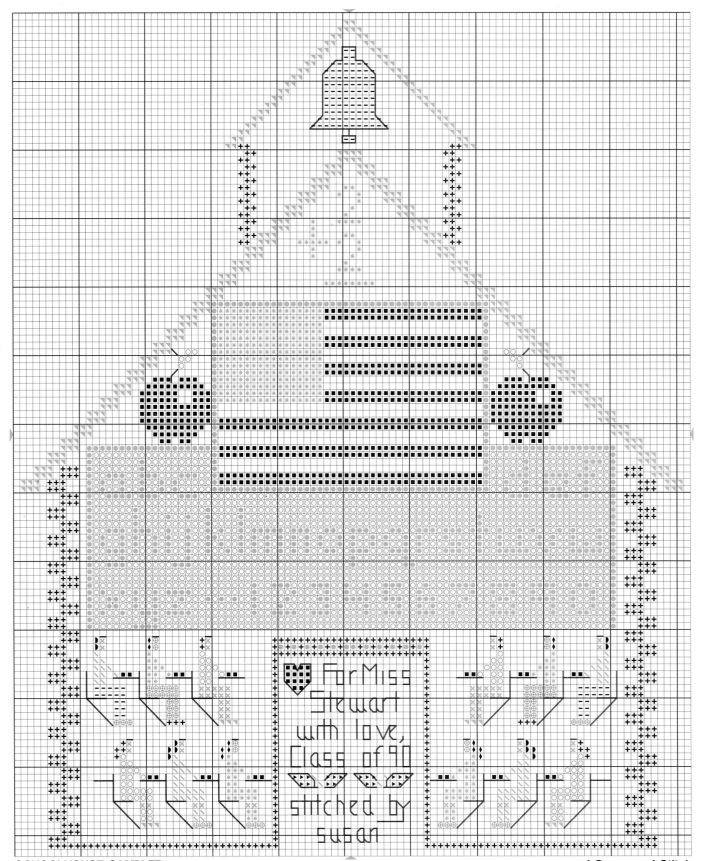

SCHOOLHOUSE SAMPLER

1 Square = 1 Stitch

A-PLUS TEACHER

Shown on page 176.
Finished size of design is 3¾x5 inches. Project is shown in an 8x10-inch oval frame.
Design is 52x70 stitches.

MATERIALS

10x12-inch piece of ecru 14-count Aida cloth
One skein of DMC embroidery floss in colors listed on the color key
Tapestry needle
Embroidery hoop

INSTRUCTIONS

The chart for the design appears on page 185.

Hem or tape raw edges of fabric to prevent threads from raveling as you work.

Measure 3½ inches down and 5 inches in from top left corner of cloth. Begin stitching the top leaf of the top apple here.

Use two strands of floss and work cross-stitches and backstitches over one thread of fabric. Work the entire center of the blackboard with the exception of the A-plus with No. 3021 brown gray. Use No. 962 pink for the A-plus. Use white floss to backstitch the remainder of the message on the blackboard.

Backstitch the blackboard, blackboard frame, chalk, and eraser with No. 310 black. Backstitch the stems on the flowers and vines and the apple stems with No. 469 green and the lettering of the teacher's name with No. 993 aqua.

Using one strand of No. 993 aqua, make a French knot for the period in the teacher's name.

Remove tape; press stitchery on back side. Frame as desired.

COLOR KEY
- ◉ **White**
- ◆ **Black 310**
- ◥ **Dark Brown 3031**
- ⊕ **Light Brown 433**
- ⊠ **Tan 950**
- − **Gray 646**
- + **Rust 919**
- ▶ **Yellow 743**
- ⊞ **Navy Blue 312**
- ◎ **Green 991**
- ■ **Red 321**
- ◺ **Magenta 718**
- ▶ **Coral 315**

SCHOOLHOUSE SAMPLER

Shown on page 177.
Finished framed size, matted as shown, is 12x14 inches.
Design is 100x121 stitches.

MATERIALS

14x16-inch piece of ecru 14-count Aida cloth
One skein of DMC embroidery floss in colors listed on the color key
Tapestry needle
Embroidery hoop

INSTRUCTIONS

The chart appears *opposite*.

Hem or tape raw edges of fabric to prevent threads from raveling as you work.

Measure 3½ inches down and 7 inches in from top left corner of cloth. Begin stitching the top stitch (point) of the schoolhouse bell tower here.

Use two strands of floss and work cross-stitches and backstitches over one thread of fabric.

Backstitch the school desks with No. 312 navy blue and the teacher's name, message, date, and student's name with No. 919 rust. Backstitch the bell with No. 310 black, the apple stems with No. 991 green, and the heart with No. 321 red.

Backstitch coral leaves under "Class of 90" with No. 351 coral. Make one backstitch across the top of each student's head using the same color as the hair.

Make 50 French knot stars on the flag using two strands of white.

Remove tape; press stitchery on back side. Frame as desired.

HALLOWEEN SHIRTS

Shown on page 181.
Designs are 7x8 stitches (spider), 8x8 stitches (ant), and 31x7 stitches (bat).

MATERIALS

Purchased sweatshirt
Pieces of 8½-count waste canvas sufficiently large for the number of motifs you wish to stitch
One skein of No. 310 black DMC embroidery floss
Tapestry needle
Embroidery hoop

INSTRUCTIONS

The spider, ant, and bat patterns for the shirts are *below*.

Any number and combination of motifs may be used. Plan your shirt before you begin stitching.

Baste waste canvas onto the front of the sweatshirt following manufacturer's directions. Use six strands of floss and work cross-stitches over one thread of waste canvas. Use four strands for backstitches.

When stitching is completed, trim the waste canvas ¼ inch past the stitching. Dampen the stitchery with warm water; gently pull threads of canvas from beneath the stitches.

When sweatshirt is dry, press with a warm iron.

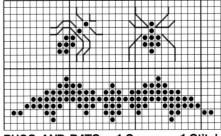

BUGS AND BATS   1 Square = 1 Stitch

COLOR KEY
- ◉ **Black 310**

PUMPKIN TREAT BAG

Shown on page 180.
Finished bag is 15x14 inches.
Design is 80x58 stitches.

MATERIALS

20x10 inches of ecru 14-count Aida
   cloth
One skein of DMC embroidery floss in
   colors listed on the color key
Tapestry needle
Embroidery hoop
1 yard of natural canvas
1 yard of orange cotton for lining
¼ yard of orange-and-black-striped
   calico for handles and piping
1 yard of cotton cording for piping
Thread
18x8-inch strip of cotton batiste
Fusible interfacing

INSTRUCTIONS

The chart for the pumpkin design appears *below.*

Tape raw edges of the Aida cloth to prevent raveling.

Locate the center of the design and the center of the fabric. Arrows on the chart mark the vertical and horizontal centers. Begin stitching here.

Use two strands of floss and work cross-stitches and backstitches over one thread of fabric.

When all cross-stitching is finished, backstitch areas indicated by solid red lines with No. 310 black.

Trim cross-stitch fabric to measure 16x6 inches, keeping pumpkin design centered. (Top and bottom edges will be 16 inches and sides will be 6 inches in length.) Cover cotton cording with piping fabric. Line cross-stitched strip with batiste and stitch piping to top and bottom edges of fabric, using ½-inch seams. Press raw edges to back side.

Use ½-inch seams throughout. Cut canvas and lining fabric to measure 16x36 inches. Cut two 3x15-inch handles from striped fabric.

Measure 7 inches down on one end of canvas fabric and draw a horizontal line across the 16-inch width. Topstitch cross-stitched strip along this line, stitching in the ditch of the piping at both top and bottom.

With right sides facing, fold canvas fabric in half to measure 16x18 inches. Sew the two sides of bag. Repeat with lining fabric, leaving an opening in one side seam of lining for turning.

To make the box corners for bottom of bag, measure 2 inches up and 2 inches in from one bottom corner of folded edge of

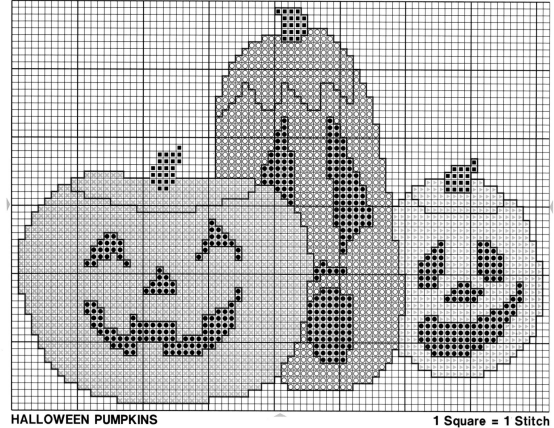

HALLOWEEN PUMPKINS

1 Square = 1 Stitch

COLOR KEY
- Black 310
- Green 905
- Dark Orange 606
- Orange 608
- Gold 741

canvas. Draw a diagonal line between the two points; machine-stitch atop drawn line; cut away excess fabric. Repeat for opposite side.

Make box corners on lining fabric.

Press interfacing to wrong side of handles. Press under ½-inch seam allowance along long edges of handles. Press handles in half lengthwise, wrong sides facing, matching folded edges; topstitch edges together. Stitch each handle to top of bag 5 inches from one side of bag.

With right sides facing, sew lining to bag along top edges, keeping handles to inside. Turn lining to right side and inside bag through opening. Stitch opening closed. Topstitch around top of bag.

Fold top of bag down approximately 2½ inches to make cuff; turn handles up toward top of bag. Topstitch bottom of cuff; topstitch handles in place along top edge of bag.

THANKSGIVING TABLECLOTH

Shown on page 183.
Finished size of cloth is 44 inches square.
Design is 13½ inches in diameter.

MATERIALS
46x46-inch piece of light brown linen with approximately 25 threads per inch (We used Floba cloth from Zweigart.)
DMC embroidery floss in colors listed on the color key; number of skeins required appears in parentheses
Tapestry needle
Embroidery hoop

INSTRUCTIONS
The chart for one quarter of the circle of leaves appears on page 190. Outlines at each end of the chart show you where to place the repeat. You will need to work the design four times to finish a complete circle.

Hem or tape raw edges of fabric to prevent threads from raveling as you work.

Find the center of the cloth. Measure down 6½ inches from this point. Begin working here. An arrow on the chart shows you where to begin.

Use two strands of floss and work the cross-stitches over two threads of fabric.

Repeat the leaf quadrant, working to the right (counterclockwise) of the previously worked section.

With one strand of No. 783 bright gold floss, use the stem stitch (see diagram, page 216) to add the long graceful lines on the heads of wheat. These lines appear in red on the chart on page 190.

Press the finished stitchery on the back side.

Fold raw edges of linen under ⅜ inch on all sides; press. Fold under another ⅜ inch; press. Machine- or hand-hem all sides.

PLACE MAT AND NAPKIN

Shown on page 182.
Finished size of place mat is 18x14 inches.
Napkin is 18 inches square.
Each vertical stem of wheat is 16 stitches wide and 77 stitches long.

MATERIALS
Light brown linen with approximately 25 threads per inch as follows: 19x15 inches for each place mat; 19-inch square for each napkin (We used Floba cloth from Zweigart.)
One skein of DMC embroidery floss in colors listed on the color key
Tapestry needle
Embroidery hoop

INSTRUCTIONS
Hem or tape raw edges of fabric to prevent threads from raveling as you work.

Use two strands of floss and work the cross-stitches over two threads of fabric.

With one strand of No. 783 bright gold floss, use the stem stitch (see diagram, page 216) to add the long graceful lines on the heads of wheat. These lines appear in red on the chart on page 191.

For the place mat
Use the entire pattern on page 191 for the place mat. Measure 6½ inches down and 3 inches in from the top left corner. Begin stitching the top cross-stitch of the vertical stem of wheat here. An arrow on the chart shows you where to begin.

For the napkin
For the napkin, use only the vertical stem of wheat on the pattern on page 191. Measure 11½ inches down and 2½ inches in from the top left corner of the napkin. Begin stitching the top stitch of the vertical stem of wheat here. An arrow on the chart shows you where to begin.

For both projects
Press the finished stitchery on the back side. Machine- or hand-stitch a ¼-inch hem on all four sides, turning edge under twice before stitching.

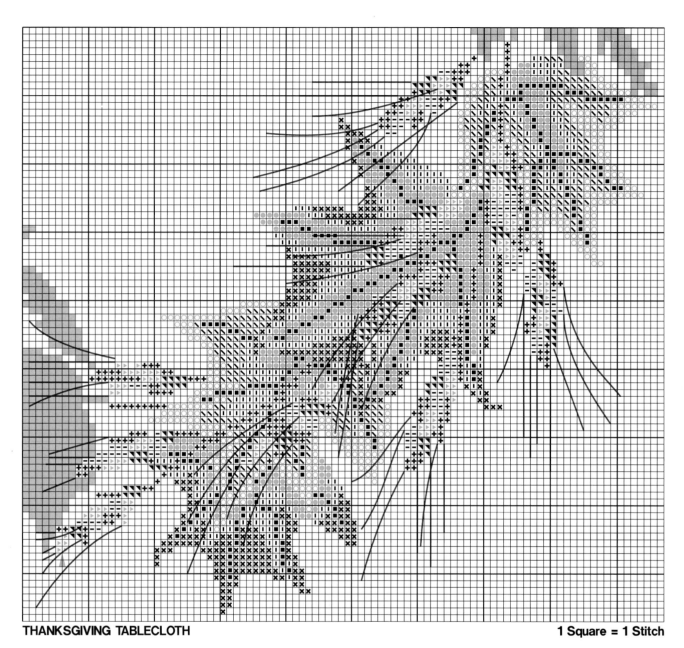

THANKSGIVING TABLECLOTH

1 Square = 1 Stitch

COLOR KEY

- ▣ Topaz 782 (1)
- ▨ Copper 919 (1)
- ⊡ Medium Copper 920 (1)
- ⊠ Olive 733 (1)
- ◩ Coral 350 (1)
- ☐ Orange 946 (2)
- ⊞ Gold 680 (1)
- ◥ Light Gold 676 (1)
- ⊟ Bright Gold 783 (2)
- ⊡ Old Gold 370 (1)

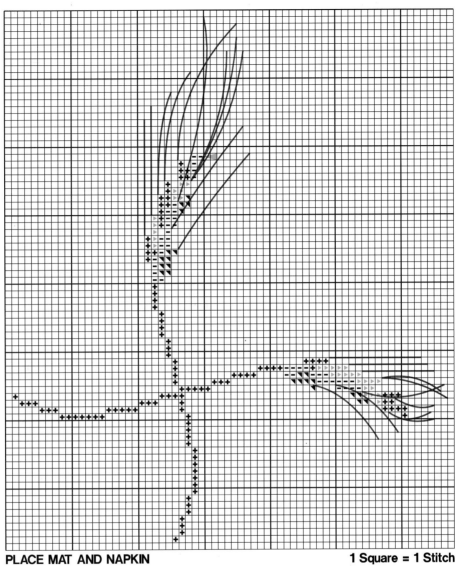

COLOR KEY
⊞ Gold 680
◥ Light Gold 676
⊟ Bright Gold 783
⊡ Old Gold 370

PLACE MAT AND NAPKIN

1 Square = 1 Stitch

Recollections of Christmastime At Home

Opening boxes of treasured ornaments, putting up holiday greens, decorating sugar cookies, and singing favorite carols—these are the ingredients of a perfect Christmas memory.

Celebrate the season with the mini-samplers, *right.* The small 2½x3½-inch designs are worked quickly on 14-count cloth and can be framed together or individually. Gold metallic thread adds a festive touch.

Trimming the tree is always a favorite family activity. The old-fashioned scene, *opposite,* depicts the true enjoyment found in holiday preparations. With lazy daisy stitches and French knots, intricate details are brought to life in the scene. And, combining two floss colors in one stitch adds texture and shading.

Instructions for these projects begin on page 203 with charts beginning on page 200.

CHERYL GRINDAHL
1988

Blessings For a Happy Holiday

To give as gifts or send as cards to cherished friends or to display in your own home, house blessings offer salutations of good cheer.

The small greetings, *left,* can be stitched quickly and used in many ways. Work the projects on perforated paper and attach each one to card stock for unique greetings that can be framed after the holidays. Or, use Aida cloth for the background and mount the finished piece in a candlestand or picture frame.

Guardian angels watch over the house and offer glad tidings in the Christmas sampler, *opposite.* Soft and subtle pastel colors, combined with metallic thread, create a look of elegance. Backstitching and French knots enhance the detail of the 9¾x19-inch wall hanging.

Instructions begin on page 208.

The Stockings Are Hung by The Chimney

Even today, we prefer traditional comforts at Christmastime. There's a tug at the heartstrings when we place an ornament from grade school on the tree or hang a stocking above the fireplace.

Your very favorite Christmas Eve visitor will welcome a snack baked in your kitchen and served on the handsome tray, *above*. The 11-inch opening holds a familiar scene worked in cross-stitch on 16-count Aida cloth.

Looking at the pillow, *opposite*, you can almost hear the familiar strains of "We Wish You a Merry Christmas." Worked on hardanger fabric with backstitches of gold metallic thread, the design here has been finished into a pillow with piping and a ruffled edge.

Instructions for the tray begin on page 210; instructions for the pillow begin on page 205.

Singing the Praises of Christmas

Freshly cut evergreens bring a wonderful aroma to our homes as we proudly display our handmade decorations.

The 5x3¾-inch ornaments, *above*, can be worked in any combination of colors using one light, four medium, and two dark shades of floss, plus a color for the lettering. Use jewel tones on ecru or pastel Aida cloth, and softer thread colors on darker fabrics.

Matted with an exquisite chintz fabric, the wall hanging, *opposite*, measures 23x26¾ inches. The cross-stitch is worked on a 25-count even-weave fabric and finished with a 5-inch-wide mat covered in your favorite fabric.

Instructions begin on page 211.

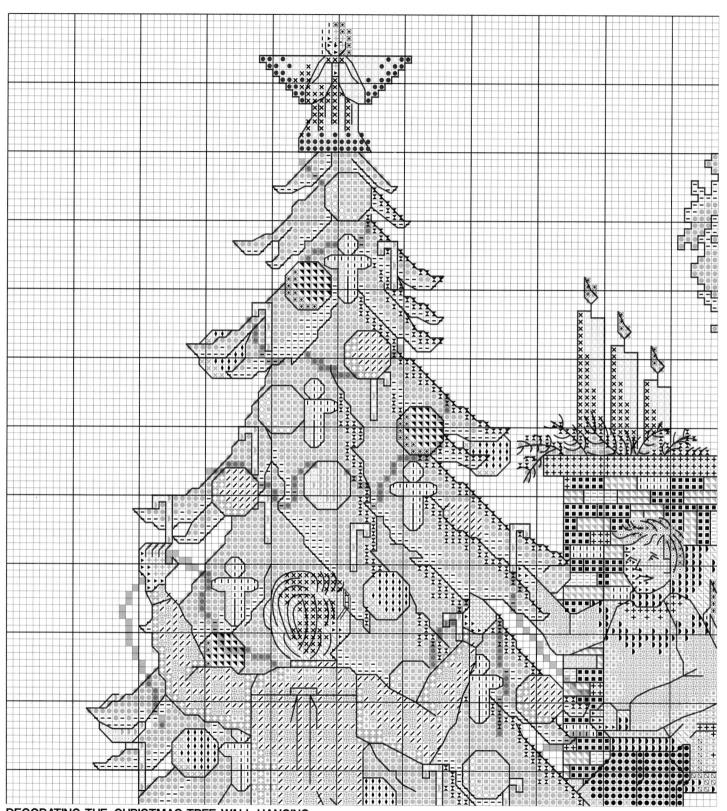

DECORATING–THE–CHRISTMAS–TREE WALL HANGING

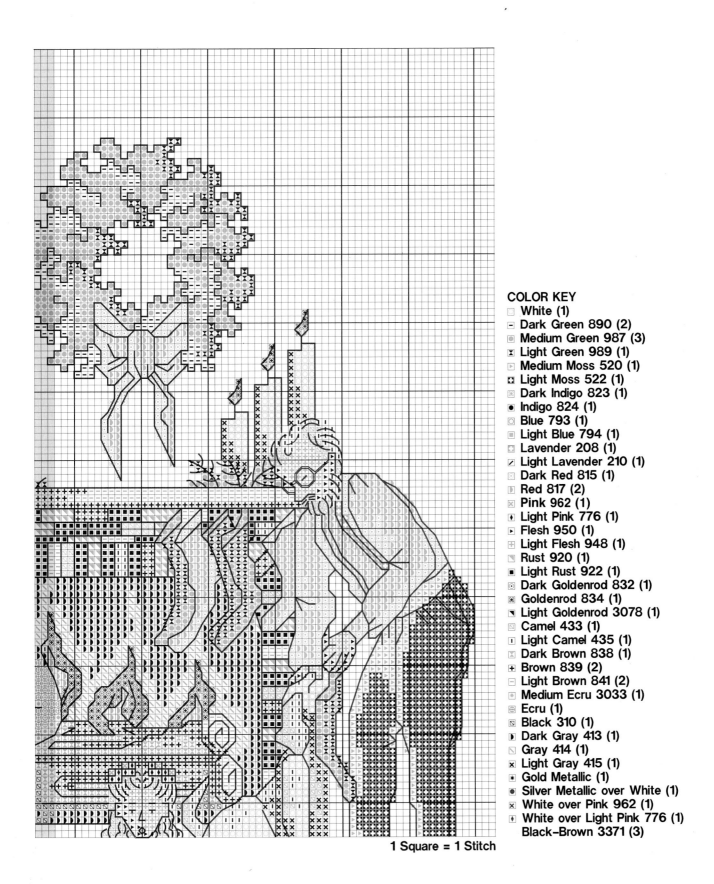

COLOR KEY

- White (1)
- Dark Green 890 (2)
- Medium Green 987 (3)
- Light Green 989 (1)
- Medium Moss 520 (1)
- Light Moss 522 (1)
- Dark Indigo 823 (1)
- Indigo 824 (1)
- Blue 793 (1)
- Light Blue 794 (1)
- Lavender 208 (1)
- Light Lavender 210 (1)
- Dark Red 815 (1)
- Red 817 (2)
- Pink 962 (1)
- Light Pink 776 (1)
- Flesh 950 (1)
- Light Flesh 948 (1)
- Rust 920 (1)
- Light Rust 922 (1)
- Dark Goldenrod 832 (1)
- Goldenrod 834 (1)
- Light Goldenrod 3078 (1)
- Camel 433 (1)
- Light Camel 435 (1)
- Dark Brown 838 (1)
- Brown 839 (2)
- Light Brown 841 (2)
- Medium Ecru 3033 (1)
- Ecru (1)
- Black 310 (1)
- Dark Gray 413 (1)
- Gray 414 (1)
- Light Gray 415 (1)
- Gold Metallic (1)
- Silver Metallic over White (1)
- White over Pink 962 (1)
- White over Light Pink 776 (1)
- Black–Brown 3371 (3)

1 Square = 1 Stitch

DECORATING-THE-CHRISTMAS-TREE WALL HANGING

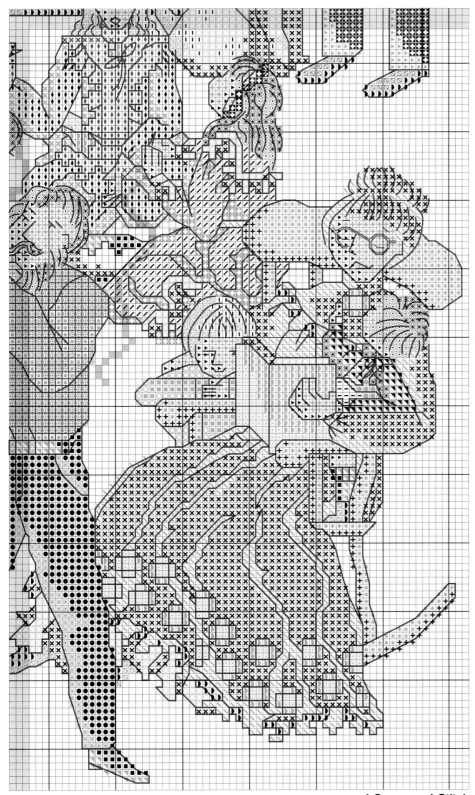

1 Square = 1 Stitch

DECORATING-THE-CHRISTMAS-TREE WALL HANGING

Shown on page 193.
Finished size of stitchery is 12¼x16 inches.
Design is 171x224 stitches.

MATERIALS

21x24-inch piece of white 14-count Aida
  cloth
DMC embroidery floss in colors listed
  on the color key on page 201;
  number of skeins required appears in
  parentheses
Silver metallic thread
Gold metallic thread
Tapestry needle
Embroidery hoop

INSTRUCTIONS

The chart for the family scene shown on
page 193 is divided into sections and
printed on pages 200–203.

Shaded areas on the chart show you
where one section of the pattern overlaps
with the next. Do not rework the shaded
areas as you move from section to section.
These areas are only a placement guide.

Hem or bind raw edges of the fabric
with masking tape.

The 21-inch measurement runs along
the top and bottom of the rectangle of
fabric and the 24-inch measurement runs
down each side.

Use three strands of floss and work
cross-stitches over one thread of fabric.
Use two strands of floss for French knots.
(See stitch diagrams, page 216.)

continued

MERRY CHRISTMAS TO ALL

Measure down 3 inches and in 5½ inches from upper left corner of fabric. Referring to chart on page 200, begin stitching top left stitch of angel's hair here.

DUPLICATE CROSS-STITCHES (indicated by red symbols on color key): Entire dress of treetop angel is worked in white and shaded with No. 415 light gray. Work a second set of cross-stitches over first using one strand of silver metallic thread.

Work daughter's entire pink dress, then make a second set of cross-stitches over those stitches using one strand of white.

BACKSTITCHES (solid red outlines on diagram): For shirt of man lifting girl, work stitches using one strand of No. 208 lavender. For beading on lace of lavender dress, work stitches with two strands of No. 817 red. For needles in hands of girls in pink and lavender dresses, work stitches with two strands of silver metallic thread. For spectacles, work stitches with two strands of gold metallic thread.

For all other outlining, work backstitches using one strand of No. 3371 black-brown.

STRAIGHT STITCHES (long solid red lines on chart): Over all blond hair, work straight stitches with one strand *each* of No. 832 dark goldenrod and No. 3371 black-brown together. Use one strand *each* of No. 433 camel and black-brown together over all brown hair, and one strand *each* of No. 414 gray and black-brown together over gray hair.

For mantel boughs, work straight stitches with one strand *each* of No. 890 dark green and black-brown together.

DAISY STITCHES (red loops on chart): For bows on little girl's hair and pink dress, work daisy stitches and straight stitches using two strands of No. 989 light green. For bow tie on boy on grandma's lap, work daisy stitches and straight stitches with two strands of No. 817 red.

For mistletoe leaves, work daisy stitches with one strand of No. 890 dark green.

FRENCH KNOTS (worked over cross-stitches): For angel's hair, work one French knot over each cross-stitch using one strand *each* of No. 832 dark goldenrod and No. 3371 black-brown together.

For hair of man with mistletoe, work one French knot over each cross-stitch using one strand *each* of No. 838 dark brown and black-brown together. For four shirt buttons on man lifting child, work French knots with two strands of black-brown.

For grandma's petticoat and petticoat under pink dress, work one French knot over each cross-stitch using two strands of white. For collar on grandma's dress, work three French knots just above left side of collar and two just above right side of collar using two strands of white.

For edging around arms and hem of pinafore of girl in the air, work French knots over each cross-stitch using two strands of white.

Work strings of popcorn on tree and in girls' laps, and popcorn in bowl with two strands of white (see red shaded symbol on chart). For mistletoe berries over head of girl at piano, work random French knots with two strands of white.

Frame as desired.

FRAMED MINI-SAMPLERS

Shown on page 192.
Finished size of each design is 2½x3½ inches.
Each design is 35x49 stitches.

MATERIALS
For each sampler
7x8-inch piece of ecru 14-count Aida cloth
One skein of DMC embroidery floss in colors listed on the color key
Gold metallic embroidery thread
Tapestry needle; embroidery hoop

INSTRUCTIONS
Charts for both designs appear at *right*.

Hem or tape raw edges of fabric to prevent threads from raveling as you work.

Measure 2 inches down and 2 inches in from top left corner of cloth. Begin stitching upper left-hand corner of border here. Use two strands of floss and work stitches over one thread of fabric.

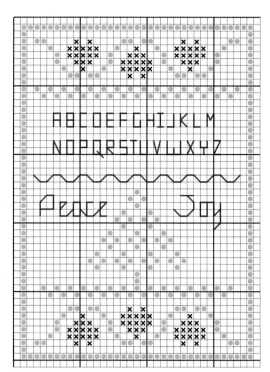

MINI–SAMPLERS   **1 Square = 1 Stitch**

COLOR KEY
◎ White
☒ Red 666
⊙ Green 701
◹ Brown 400

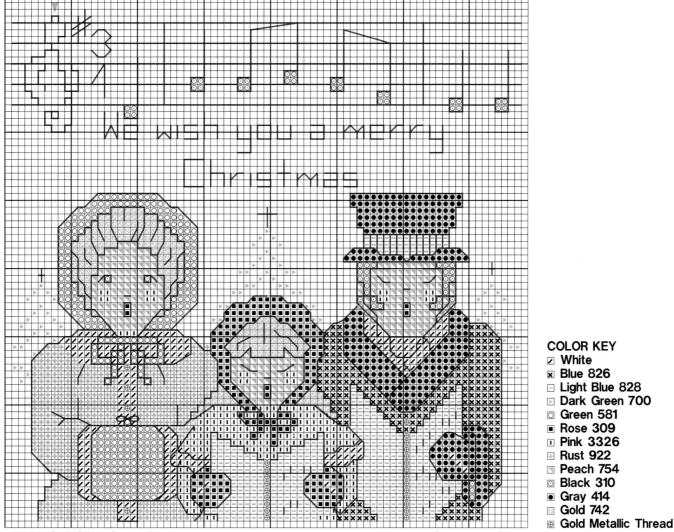

MERRY CHRISTMAS PILLOW

COLOR KEY
- ☑ White
- ☒ Blue 826
- ☐ Light Blue 828
- ⊡ Dark Green 700
- ⊚ Green 581
- ◼ Rose 309
- ⊡ Pink 3326
- ⊞ Rust 922
- ◨ Peach 754
- ◎ Black 310
- ● Gray 414
- ⬓ Gold 742
- ⊕ Gold Metallic Thread

1 Square = 1 Stitch

FRENCH KNOTS: Beginning with red, alternate two strands of No. 666 red and No. 701 green for French knot flowers in the bouquet on the angels sampler. Dot the letter "i" with No. 666 red. Using red, add French knot berries above and below the vine on the Peace sampler. (Refer to photograph on page 192.)

BACKSTITCHES: Use two strands of No. 701 green for the vine above the tree, the words "Peace" and "Joy," the stems on angels' bouquet, and border. Use No. 666 red to stitch around the angels' dresses, "Christmas 1991", and alphabets. Backstitch around the wings with one strand of gold metallic thread.

Remove tape; press stitchery on wrong side. Frame as desired.

MERRY CHRISTMAS PILLOW

Shown on page 197.
Finished size of pillow shown, including ruffle, is 13x15 inches.
Design is 77x77 stitches.

MATERIALS
15x15-inch piece of ecru hardanger fabric
One skein of DMC embroidery floss in colors listed on the color key
Gold metallic thread
1½ yards of purchased piping
1½ yards of backing and ruffle fabric
Polyester fiberfill
Embroidery hoop
Tapestry needle

INSTRUCTIONS
The chart for the pillow appears *above.*

Hem or tape raw edges of fabric to prevent threads from raveling as you work.

Measure down 4 inches from the top and 4 inches in from the left side and begin stitching the musical score here. (The arrow shows you where to begin.)

Use three strands of floss for cross-stitches and two strands for backstitches. Work stitches over two threads of fabric.

The woman's coat buttons and the songbooks' bindings are cross-stitched with gold metallic thread. Stars on treetops and musical score are backstitched
continued on page 208

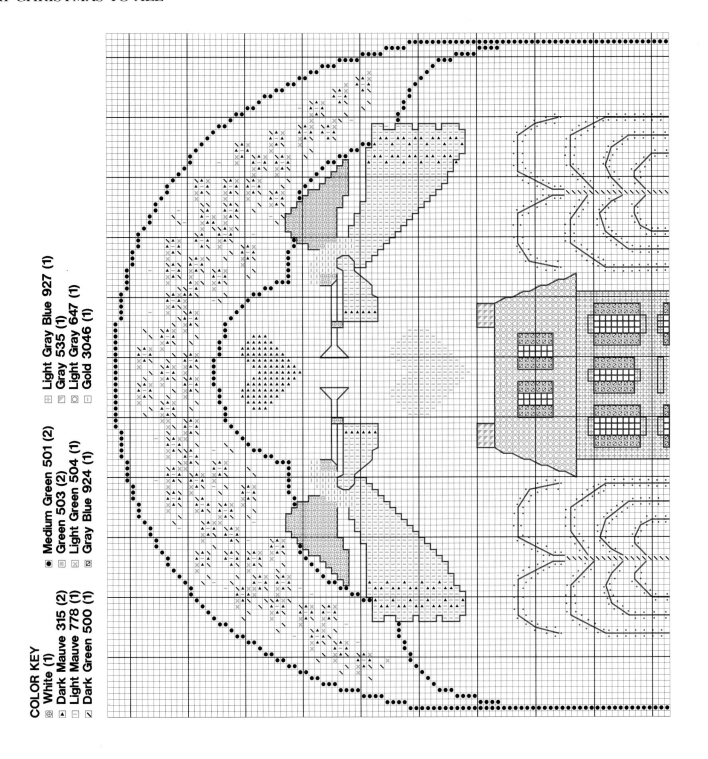

COLOR KEY
⊕ White (1)
▲ Dark Mauve 315 (2)
– Light Mauve 778 (1)
◣ Dark Green 500 (1)

● Medium Green 501 (2)
▫ Green 503 (2)
☒ Light Green 504 (1)
☑ Gray Blue 924 (1)

⊞ Light Gray Blue 927 (1)
◪ Gray 535 (1)
◎ Light Gray 647 (1)
▫ Gold 3046 (1)

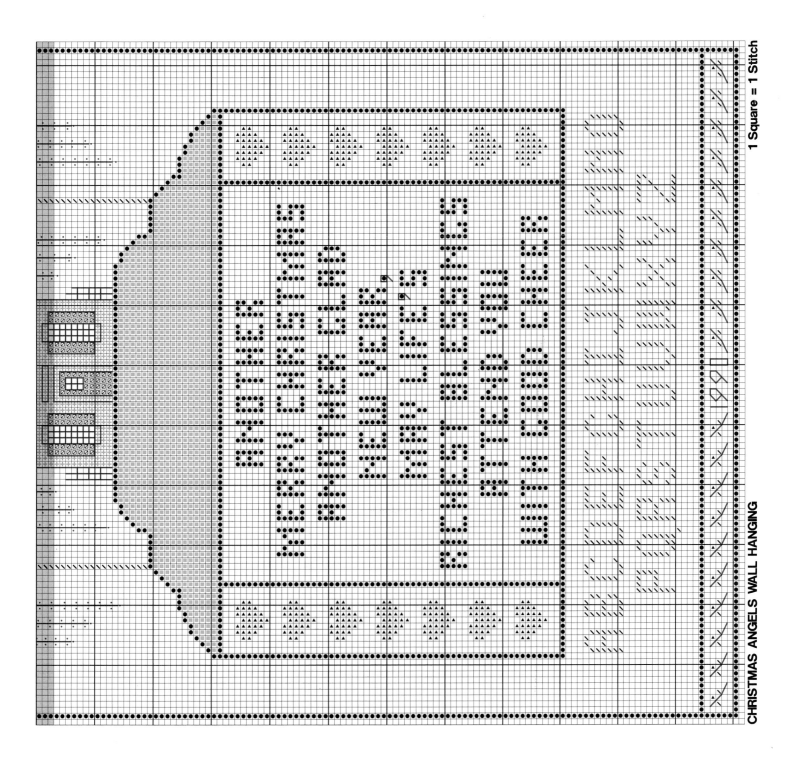

CHRISTMAS ANGELS WALL HANGING

continued from page 205
with gold metallic thread. The treble clef sign, sharp sign, stems of notes, numbers 3 and 4, and outlines of clothes and faces are backstitched with two strands of No. 310 black. Words are backstitched with two strands of No. 309 rose.

Use two strands of rose to make French knots above letter "i" in words.

Use two strands of No. 581 green to make two daisy stitches for the bow on the top of the woman's muff. Stitch diagrams appear on page 216.

Remove tape from finished stitchery. Press on back side. Finish as desired.

CHRISTMAS ANGELS WALL HANGING

Shown on page 195.
Finished size is 9¾x19 inches.
Design is 112x214 stitches.

MATERIALS
16x25-inch piece of hardanger fabric
DMC embroidery floss in colors listed on the color key; number of skeins required appears in parentheses
Silver metallic thread
Tapestry needle
Embroidery hoop

INSTRUCTIONS
The chart for this design is on pages 206 and 207 and is divided into two parts. The shaded rows of stitches on page 207 are repeated from page 206 and are used to guide you in moving from one section to the next. Do not restitch these rows.

Hem or tape raw edges of fabric to prevent threads from raveling as you work.

Measure 3 inches up and 3 inches in from the bottom left corner of the cloth. Begin stitching the lower left of the bor-

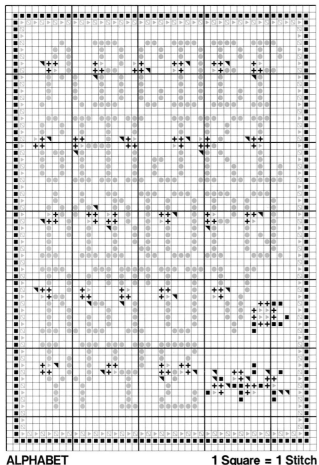

ALPHABET   1 Square = 1 Stitch

COLOR KEY
- ■ Aqua 958
- ▨ Light Aqua 964
- ▷ Pink 600
- ⊞ Light Pink 3354
- ▨ Dark Green 699
- ◣ Light Green 704

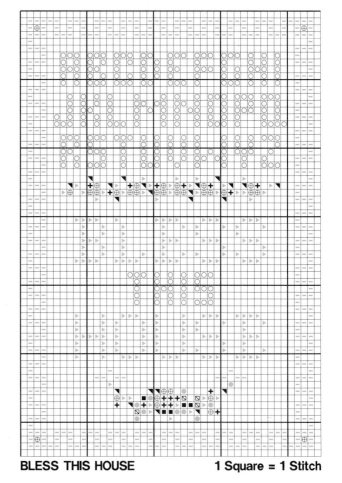

BLESS THIS HOUSE   1 Square = 1 Stitch

COLOR KEY
- ▷ Burgundy 814
- ⊟ Blue 826
- ⊞ Pink 600
- ⊕ Medium Pink 603
- ▯ Light Pink 3354
- ▨ Dark Green 699
- ◣ Green 704
- ▨ Purple 553
- ■ Gold 972

der here. Work all stitches over two threads of fabric. Use three strands of floss for cross-stitches. Use one strand of No. 315 dark mauve for backstitching faces and hands. Use two strands for all remaining backstitches as follows:

Backstitch the angels' wings in No. 778 light mauve and the dresses in No. 315 dark mauve. Backstitch the house in No. 924 gray-blue and the roof and fence in No. 535 gray. Backstitch the branches of the trees, the date, and the flower stems at the bottom with No. 500 dark green.

Backstitch punctuation marks with No. 501 medium green. Backstitch trumpets with silver metallic thread.

Use two strands of No. 500 dark green for the French knot leaves on the trees.

Remove tape from stitchery; press stitchery on wrong side using a damp cloth and warm iron. Frame as desired.

MINI-SAMPLERS

Shown on page 194.
Finished design areas are 3x4½ inches.
Designs are approximately 45x65 stitches.

MATERIALS

5x7 inches of ivory perforated paper (available in crafts and needlework stores) or 14-count Aida cloth
One 9½x6-inch piece of card-stock paper in the color of your choice (for one card)
Or, one candlestand frame with 3½x5-inch insert designed for needlework (available through needlework shops)
One skein of DMC embroidery floss in colors listed on the color key
Tapestry needle
Glue stick

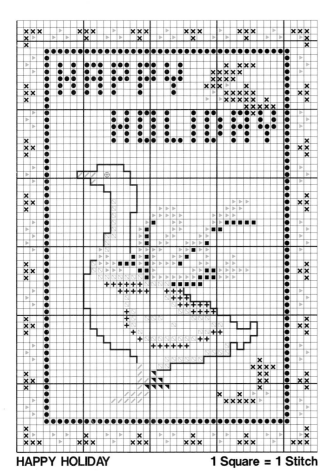

HAPPY HOLIDAY   **1 Square = 1 Stitch**

COLOR KEY
- ◼ Burgundy 498
- ▷ Red 666
- ◣ Orange 740
- ▨ Light Orange 741
- ⊞ Tan 738
- ▨ Beige 739
- ● Dark Green 699
- ⊠ Green 701
- ⊕ Gray 648

CHRISTMAS PAST   **1 Square = 1 Stitch**

COLOR KEY
- ⊠ Green 701
- ▷ Red 666

continued

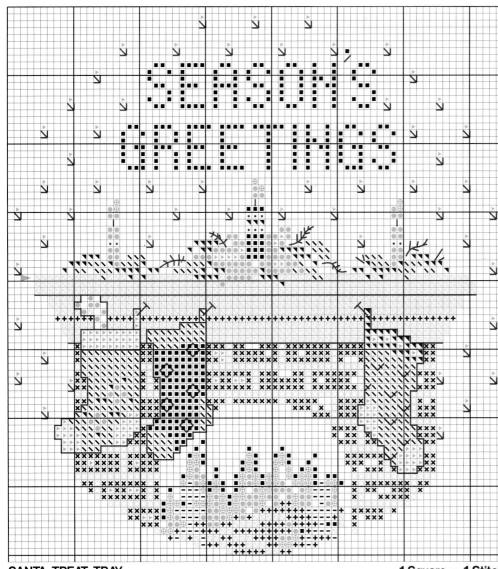

SANTA TREAT TRAY

COLOR KEY
- ■ Blue 826
- ⊠ Barn Red 498
- ◉ Red 321
- ▷ Pink 957
- ◥ Dark Green 700
- ◢ Light Green 704
- ⊞ Dark Brown 433
- ▨ Brown 436
- − Black 310
- □ Gray 318
- ⊕ Gold 742

1 Square = 1 Stitch

INSTRUCTIONS

Charts for the cards/framed samplers appear on pages 208 and 209.

Locate the center of the design and the center of the perforated paper or Aida cloth; begin stitching here. Use two strands of floss to work cross-stitches over one square of the paper or thread of cloth.

BACKSTITCHING: For "Happy Holiday" design, work backstitches on goose using two strands of No. 648 gray. Work lettering on "Memories of Christmas Past" sampler and lines on border using two strands of No. 701 green.

FINISHING CARDS: Trim the perforated paper to within four squares beyond the stitched border. Fold the card-stock paper in half widthwise. Apply glue to the back of the stitched piece and fasten to center front of folded card or tag. Place a book or heavy object over the glued card or gift tag until the glue has dried.

FINISHING FRAMED SAMPLER: Trim the fabric leaving a 2-inch border all around design. Insert in candlestand.

SANTA TREAT TRAY

Shown on page 196.
Finished size of design is approximately 10 inches in diameter.
Design is 73x79 stitches.

MATERIALS

Round tray with 11-inch-diameter insert designed for needlework (available at needlework shops)
15x15-inch piece of ecru 16-count Aida cloth
One skein of DMC embroidery floss in colors listed on the color key
Gold metallic thread
Tapestry needle; embroidery hoop

INSTRUCTIONS

The plate/tray shown on page 196 is from Sudberry House, Old Lyme, Conn. The opening measures 11 inches in diameter. Hem or tape raw edges of fabric to prevent threads from raveling as you work.

The pattern, *opposite,* has an arrow on the left side of the fireplace to indicate where to begin stitching the design. Measure down 7½ inches and in 3 inches from the upper left corner of the fabric. Begin stitching here. Use three strands of floss and work all cross-stitches and backstitches over two threads of fabric.

Backstitch stockings, nails holding stockings, and wicks of candles with two strands of No. 310 black.

Backstitch evergreen branches and mantel using two strands of No. 433 dark brown. Use three strands of No. 704 light green for backstitches on flower stems on background. Backstitch squares on middle stocking and candy cane with No. 321 red. Use three strands of No. 700 dark green for V-shapes on far right stocking.

Use No. 742 gold to cross-stitch the candle and fire flames, then make a second cross-stitch over the gold stitches using one strand of gold metallic thread.

Stitch French knots (red dots) on outside candles with two strands of No. 700 dark green and knots on middle candle with No. 742 gold.

Press the finished stitchery on the back side. Mount the stitchery in the tray following the manufacturer's instructions.

JOY AND NOEL
TREE ORNAMENTS

Shown on page 198.
Each finished ornament is 5x3¾ inches.
Each design is 66x46 stitches.

MATERIALS
For one ornament
8x6 inches of 14-count Aida cloth
Embroidery floss in one light, one
    contrasting, four medium, and two
    dark shades that complement the Aida
    cloth chosen
Tapestry needle; embroidery hoop
5½x4¼ inches of backing fabric
⅝ yard of piping
Polyester fiberfill
½ yard of ⅜-inch-wide ribbon

continued

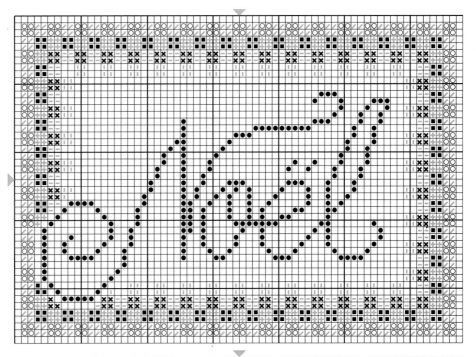

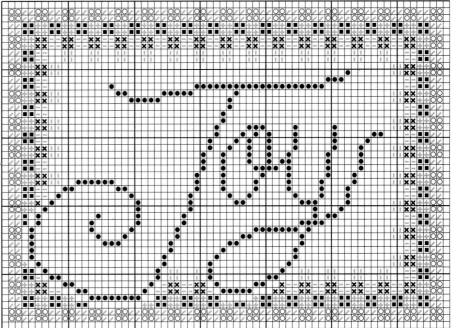

TREE ORNAMENTS   **1 Square = 1 Stitch**

COLOR KEY

⊡ Light	☒ Medium
◉ Contrast	⊟ Medium
⊠ Medium	◼ Dark
⊙ Medium	⊞ Dark

INSTRUCTIONS

Locate the center of the patterns on page 211 and the center of the fabric. Arrows on the charts mark horizontal and vertical centers. Begin stitching here.

Use three strands of floss and work cross-stitches over one thread of fabric. Select floss from favorite color families in light, medium, and dark shades with one color that is a contrast for the lettering.

Trim stitched piece to six spaces from the outer border of design on all sides.

Machine-stitch piping to cross-stitched front, leaving two spaces between border and seam. Fold ribbon in half widthwise; baste center fold to top center of ornament front, leaving ends free for tying ornament to tree.

With right sides facing and keeping ribbon free from seams, sew backing to front along piping stitch line; leave a 2-inch opening for turning. Turn right side out; stuff firmly with fiberfill.

Slip-stitch opening closed.

PINE TREE SAMPLER

Shown on page 199.
Finished size of stitchery is 13x16¾ inches.
Framed, as shown, the wall hanging is 23x26¾ inches.
Design is 163x209 stitches.

MATERIALS

25x29 inches of 25-count ecru Laguna
   even-weave fabric
DMC embroidery floss in colors listed
   on the color key; number of skeins
   required appears in parentheses
Tapestry needle
Embroidery hoop
23x26¾ inches of mat board
29x33 inches of floral fabric
Fusible webbing or spray glue

continued

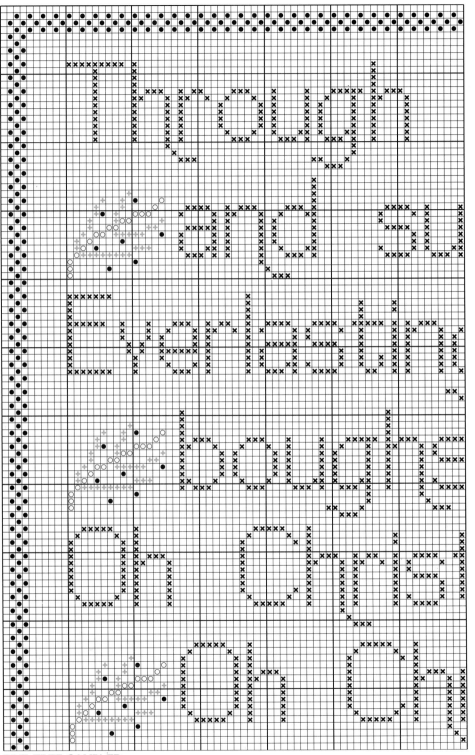

PINE TREE SAMPLER

COLOR KEY
⊠ Dark Garnet 814 (3)   ⊞ Olive 522 (1)   ◉ Light Salmon 761 (1)
                          ⊡ Dark Olive 520 (1)

1 Square = 1 Stitch

INSTRUCTIONS

The chart for the sampler is divided into four sections on pages 212–215. The shaded rows on the chart show you where the sections overlap. Do not rework the shaded rows as you move from section to section. These areas are only placement guides.

Hem or tape raw edges of fabric to prevent threads from raveling as you work. Use three strands of floss and work all cross-stitches over two threads of fabric.

Measure 6 inches down and 6 inches in from the top left corner of the cloth. Begin stitching the upper left-hand corner of the border here.

Note: Diagonal slashes shown on commas and apostrophe represent half-cross-stitches. Stitch only the first half of a cross-stitch (from lower left to upper right). See the stitch diagram on page 216.

When stitching is complete, remove tape. Press stitchery on back side, using a damp cloth and warm iron.

To mat as shown on page 199, cut a mat board 23x26¾ inches. Measure in 5 inches on all four sides. Cut inside opening. Attach mat board to wrong side of fabric with fusible webbing or spray glue. Slash an X from corner to corner of the mat opening. Turn fabric to wrong side; tape in place. Turn outer edges of fabric to back of mat board; tape in place. Frame as desired.

COLOR KEY
⊠ **Dark Garnet 814 (3)**
⊞ **Olive 522 (1)**
⊙ **Dark Olive 520 (1)**
⊡ **Light Salmon 761 (1)**

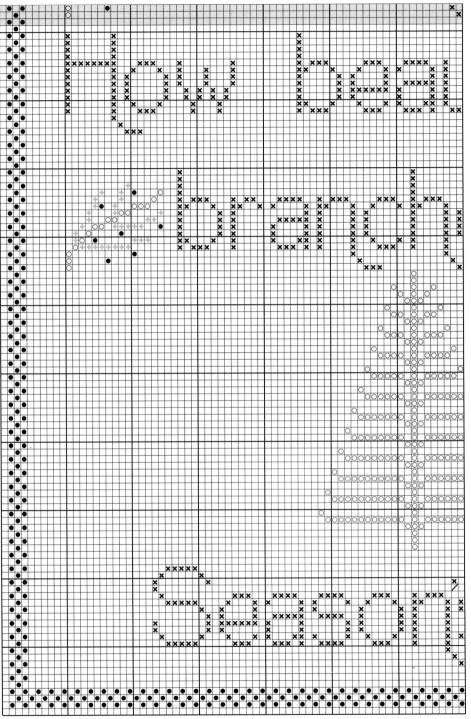

PINE TREE SAMPLER

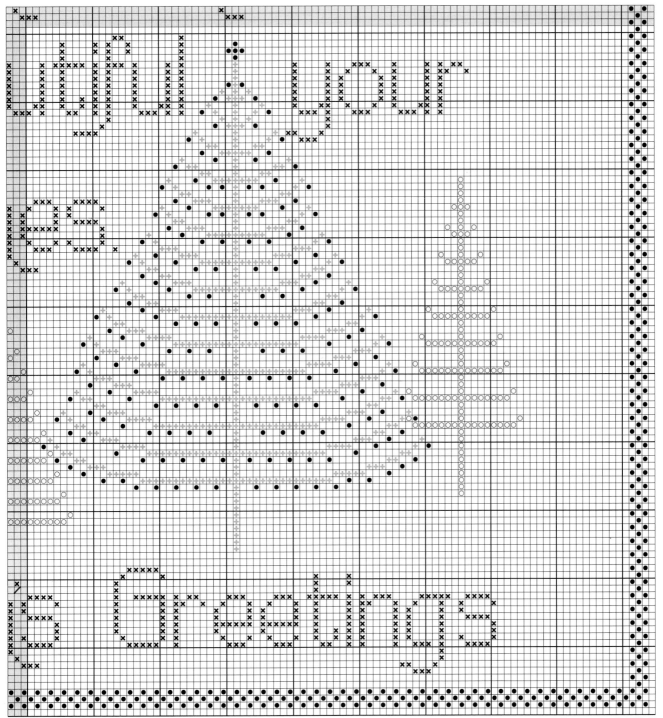

1 Square = 1 Stitch

215

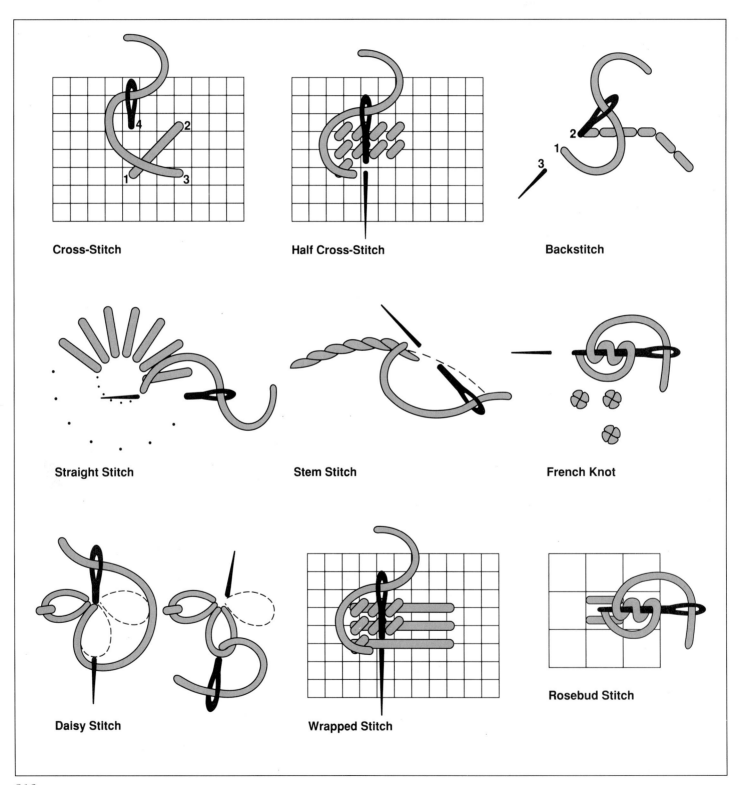

Cross-Stitch

Half Cross-Stitch

Backstitch

Straight Stitch

Stem Stitch

French Knot

Daisy Stitch

Wrapped Stitch

Rosebud Stitch

In addition to color of fabrics, the choice of fiber type and texture has broadened. Instructions for each pattern in this book specify a particular type of fabric. You may want to substitute a different color or texture of cloth to meet your own personal needs. If so, consider how the changes will affect the overall look of the cross-stitches and finished project.

Be sure to purchase adequate amounts of fabric and floss. Colors may vary slightly with each dye lot. If you are in doubt, a salesperson in the crafts store should be able to assist you with selections.

Testing for colorfastness

If you have selected deep-colored fabric or thread, it is a good idea to check for colorfastness. Although most materials will not bleed, occasionally some do. For this reason it is worthwhile to take the necessary precautions. You can set dyes simply by dipping fabric or floss into a weak solution of salt and water or vinegar and water.

When the fabric is dry, press it carefully with a damp cloth and warm iron. Hem or tape the raw edges to prevent threads from fraying as you embroider the design.

Working with floss

Six-strand embroidery floss comes in a wide variety of colors, including variegated shades.

Floss is spun so that the six strands can be separated easily. The number of strands used for a particular design depends upon the number of threads of fabric that each stitch is worked over.

Instructions for each pattern in this book will tell you how many strands of floss to use for the project shown.

When working with your own designs, use the following as a general guide: Use three strands of floss when working on 11-count fabric. Use only two strands when using smaller than 11-count.

continued

Choosing the materials

To ensure uniformity of each stitch, counted cross-stitch is worked on even-weave fabrics or perforated paper. Even-weave fabrics feature horizontal and vertical threads that are of the same thickness and that are uniformly spaced. This results in fabric with a consistent thread count at any point along its length or width.

Hardanger fabric has 22 threads per inch. If stitching over one thread, you will be able to make 22 cross-stitches per inch. When stitching over two threads, you will make 11 cross-stitches per inch. Aida cloth is available in 6, 8, 11, 14, 16, and 18 threads per inch. Linen and other even-weave fabrics vary in thread count.

Perforated paper has 14 squares to the inch with a hole (perforation) at each corner of the square. You must be careful that you do not pull the stitches too taut. This will tear the paper and leave a hole in your stitchery.

Once limited to white and ecru, even-weave fabrics and perforated papers today are available in a rainbow of colors.

CROSS-STITCH BASICS

Stitching the design
Determine where you begin stitching; this varies depending upon the design. Most often, the center or the upper left corner is the best place to start. Beginning in a corner is appropriate if you are certain of the finished size of your project. Mark the starting point with a tailor's tack or a water-erasable pen. Each project in this book tells you how to find the starting point for that project.

Be sure to allow extra fabric around the design for framing. You may wish to leave a border of plain fabric around the stitchery when you frame it, and you must allow excess fabric for stretching the stitchery around the backing.

Mount the fabric in a hoop, on stretcher strips, or in a frame, keeping the surface taut.

Making the cross-stitch
To make a cross-stitch, pull the threaded needle from the wrong side of the fabric through a hole in the even-weave fabric. If you are directed to work each cross-stitch over two threads of fabric, carry the needle across two threads and up two threads and insert it in the upper right corner.

The second stitch begins two threads below the upper right corner stitch; bring the needle up through the fabric at this point. Carry the needle across two threads and up two threads and insert it into the fabric at the upper left corner, finishing the stitch. *Note:* The number of threads a cross-stitch is worked over may vary from project to project. See the project instructions for specific directions.

You may also embroider cross-stitches in the reverse direction; work whichever direction feels more comfortable to you. The important point to remember is that stitches should be embroidered uniformly. That is, always work the top half of the cross-stitch in the same direction.

When using three strands for cross-stitches, use two strands for backstitches. When using two strands for cross-stitches, use one strand for backstitches that are worked over cross-stitches. You will, however, need to use two strands for backstitching letters, numbers, or any areas where no cross-stitches appear.

Cut thread into lengths that are comfortable to work with; 18 inches is a good length. However, you may want to cut unusual flosses, such as rayons, silks, or metallics, into shorter lengths to make stitching easier. Experiment with threads on scrap fabric before cutting lengths.

Knot any cut strands loosely together and mark them with the appropriate color number for storage.

Beginning and ending the stitch

The best way to begin a cross-stitch is by using a waste knot. It is a temporary knot and will be clipped when no longer needed. To begin, thread your needle and knot the end of your thread. Insert the needle into the right side of the fabric, about four inches away from the placement of the first cross-stitch. Bring the needle up through the fabric and work the first series of stitches. To finish the thread, slip the threaded needle under previously stitched threads on the wrong side of the fabric for 1 to 1½ inches. (You may want to weave the thread back and forth a few times.) Clip the thread.

Turn the piece to the right side and clip the waste knot. Rethread the needle with excess floss, push the needle through to the wrong side of the stitchery, and finish as directed above.

Using charts

The charts in this book feature symbols, each one representing a cross-stitch worked in a particular color. The symbols are coded in the "color key" that accompanies the chart. Each symbol on the grid represents one stitch, unless specified otherwise in the instructions.

A shaded area on a pattern extending to another page simply means that area is already represented on the other section. Use the shaded areas as guidelines to join the two sections together.

A red dot signifies placement for a French knot. The color of floss used for the French knot will be designated in the instructions for the project.

Red lines indicate backstitching (outline stitching). Floss colors will be given in the instructions.

Any unusual markings on the pattern for decorative stitches will be explained in the how-to that accompanies the pattern.

Using checkpoints

Double-check the placement of your stitches periodically and correct your work as you go. This will prevent unnecessary ripping out later on. This is especially important when working with dark threads on light fabric, because dark threads may leave stains that show if threads are removed.

Examine your work to make sure the cross-stitches are complete stitches; make sure the top stitch of each cross is worked in the same direction throughout.

If you are working a border pattern, stitch the basics of the border first to make sure your counting is accurate; add decorative portions later.

Correcting mistakes

Regardless of a stitcher's skill, mistakes are inevitable.

Small errors, such as working one or two additional stitches within a shaded area or stitching the end of a leaf so it points in a different direction, will usually go unnoticed.

Some errors, however, will spoil the design. When you've stitched around a border and the corners don't align, there's little choice but to find the error and rework the stitches.

To remove stitches, use a pair of sharp scissors with tiny blades. Working from the back side, carefully snip away the threads and discard them. Use a pair of tweezers to pluck away stubborn threads.

Cleaning the finished stitchery

Even the most careful stitcher will find it difficult to keep a cross-stitch project perfectly clean. However, these special tips will help keep your work clean as you stitch.

Wash your hands frequently to prevent body oils from staining the fabric or embroidery.

Remove your embroidery from the hoop each time you stop stitching to prevent hoop marks from soiling your fabric.

Store your project in a bag or workbasket when you are not stitching to protect it from dust or spills.

Always wash each embroidery project separately—do not wash an embroidered piece with other embroidery projects or other laundry items. Dissolve mild laundry detergent in cold water. Add the stitchery to the water and gently squeeze the suds through the fabric.

Rinse embroidery several times in clear cold water. If water becomes colored when washing embroidery, change to clean water and continue rinsing project until water remains clear.

Roll the embroidery between two clean towels, squeezing gently without wringing. *Do not* allow the embroidered piece to touch itself. Unroll towels and spread piece flat on another towel to dry. Do not leave damp embroidery folded or in a heap.

To iron your project, place the dry embroidery facedown between two clean towels and press with a warm (not hot) iron. To remove creases or fold lines from your embroidery, you may find it necessary to use the steam setting on your iron.

Do not dry-clean your embroidery unless you are stitching on wool. There is a slight chance that a reaction could occur between the thread dyes and the dry-cleaning chemicals.

ACKNOWLEDGMENTS

We would like to extend our thanks to the designers who contributed to this book. When more than one project appears on a page, the acknowledgment cites both the specific project and the page number. A page number alone indicates that one designer provided all of the projects on that page.

We also would like to give special thanks to the photographers, whose creative talents and technical skills added much to the book.

We are happy to acknowledge our gratitude to the many companies, homeowners, country inns, and historical locations that contributed to the production of this book.

DESIGNERS

Taresia Boernke—85

Gary Boling—198; 199

Laura Holtorf Collins—41–43

Sue Cornelison—66; 86–87; 154; 177–179

Laurie Craven—22–23; 70–71; 192; 194, card, *upper left;* 195

Cheryl Drivdahl—6–13; 193

Dixie Falls—44–45; 108–111; 152; 155; 167; 180–181; 194, cards, *bottom* and *upper right*

Donna Gallagher—90–91

Donna Vermillion Giampa—64–65; 68

Diane Hayes—24, sampler, *lower left;* 164–165

Rebecca Jerdee—39; 67; 119

Rebecca Jerdee and Carla Johnson— 166

Nancy Reames—46–47

Margaret Sindelar—88–89

Patricia Sparks—120

Virginia Todd-Hall—162–163

Ellen Tucker—38

Susan Viegulis—138–139

Tina Watson for DMC—69; 176; 196–197

James A. Williams—116–118; 140–143; 182–183

Dee Wittmack—25; 153

PHOTOGRAPHERS

Craig Anderson—109; 116–117; 167; 194

Sean Fitzgerald—140–143

Hopkins Associates—12–13; 22–24; 39– 42; 45, *bottom;* 46; 64–68; 84–86; 88–90; 108; 110–111; 138–139; 152; 154–155; 162–163; 178–183; 195– 198

M. Jensen Photography—8–11; 25; 38; 43–44; 45, *top;* 47; 66; 69–71; 87; 91; 119–121; 153; 164–166; 176– 177; 192–193

Perry Struse—6–7; 118

ACKNOWLEDGMENTS

Ankeny Community School District
  Ankeny, IA

Anne Brinkley Designs
  21 Ransom Rd.
  Newton Centre, MA 02159

Bauder Ice Cream
  3802 Ingersoll
  Des Moines, IA 50312

Bevington House
  Madison County Historical Society
  Winterset, IA 50273

C.M. Offray & Son, Inc.
  261 Madison Ave.
  New York, NY 10016

Charles Craft
  P.O. Box 1049
  Laurinburg, NC 28352

The Christopher Inn
  201 Mill St.
  Excelsior, MN 55331

Covington Fabrics Corp.
  McColl, SC 29570

DMC Corporation
  107 Trumbull St.
  Elizabeth, NJ 07206

Mr. and Mrs. Roger Dahlstrom

Dot's Frame Shoppe
  4521 Fleur Dr.
  Des Moines, IA 50321

Mr. and Mrs. Jim Forbes

A Homespun Heart
  810 Bluffwood Dr.
  Iowa City, IA 52245

Iowa State Fair

Janlynn Corp.
  34 Front St.
  Indian Orchard, MA 01151

Mr. and Mrs. James Laurel

Pioneer Hi-Bred International

Plain n' Fancy
  P.O. Box 357
  Mathews, VA 23109

Darrell Shull

Margaret Sindelar

Sudberry House
  Colton Rd.
  Old Lyme, CT 06371

Mr. and Mrs. Michael Treinen

Waverly Fabrics and Wall Coverings
  Division of Schumacher & Co.
  79 Madison Ave.
  New York, NY 10016

Wichelt Imports, Inc.
  R.R. 1
  Stoddard, WI 54658

Yarn Tree Designs
  117 Alexander Avenue
  Ames, IA 50010

Linda Youngquist

Zweigart Fabrics and Canvas
  Rose Gardens
  P.O. Box 261
  Madison, TN 37115

INDEX

Page numbers in **bold** type refer to pictures with accompanying text. The remaining numbers refer to how-to instructions.

A

"ABC's of Country" wall hanging, **166**, 175
"Adjust Our Sails" wall hanging, **91**, 106
Album cover, "Welcome Guest," **39**, 51
Angels, Christmas, wall hanging with, **195**, 208–209
A-plus teacher design, **176**, 187
Apple-picking family scene, **12**, 20
Apron, blue-ribbon pickles, **143**, 146
Autumn family scene, **12**, 20
Autumn pillows, **162**, 169, 171
Autumn table linens, **182**, **183**, 189

B

Baby items
  bibs
    "chew chew," **155**, 161
    Easter **84**, 97
  birth announcement pillow, **152**, 159
  birth sampler, **153**, 156
  door sign, **154**, 159
Bags
  gift, **121**, 133
  purse, floral, **89**, 100–101
  treat, pumpkin, **180**, 188–189
Band, ribbon, for jar, **142**, 146
Basket, picnic, liberty/freedom, **138**, 144
Basket border, **86**, 100
Bellpull, floral **68**, 80, 82
Bibs, baby
  "chew chew," **155**, 161
  Easter, **84**, 97
Birds, circle of, table insert with, **64**, 72
Birth announcement pillow, **152**, 159
Birth sampler, **153**, 156
Blanket border, pheasant, **165**, 171–172
"Bless This Boat" wall hanging, **91**, 105
"Bless This Farm" wall hanging, **167**, 175
Blue-ribbon pickles apron, **143**, 146

Boat scenes
  "Adjust Our Sails," **91**, 106
  "Bless This Boat," **91**, 105
  porthole with sailboats, **90**, 106
Book covers
  "Decorate with Stitches," **88**, 102
  "Welcome Guest," **39**, 51
Borders
  flower basket, **86**, 100
  pheasant, for blanket, **165**, 171–172
Boxes, jewelry
  with monogram, **69**, 82
  pheasant, **164**, 171–172
  shamrock, **46**, 58, 61
Boy's overalls with roller coaster motif, **140**, 148, 150
Bunny, Easter, **85**, 92, 94, 96

C

Candlestands and cards, mini-samplers for, **194**, 209–210
"The Cat Did It" wall hanging, **45**, 61
Charts and checkpoints, using, 219
Cherries dresser jar insert, **45**, 58
"Chew chew" baby bib, **155**, 161
Children's items
  Easter bunny, **85**, 92, 94, 96
  overalls, boy's, with roller coaster motif, **140**, 148, 150
  overalls, girl's, with ice-cream cones, **140**, 150
  sweatshirt inserts, dinosaur and falling star, **178**, **179**, 184–185
  sweatshirts, Halloween, **181**, 187
  treat bag, pumpkin, **180**, 188–189
  See also Baby items
Christmas items
  angels wall hanging, **195**, 208–209
  decorating-the-Christmas-tree wall hanging, **193**, 203–204
  mini-samplers
    for cards or candlestand, **194**, 209–210
    framed, **192**, 204–205
  pillow, Merry Christmas, **197**, 205, 208
  pine tree sampler, **199**, 212, 214
  Santa treat tray, **196**, 210–211
  tree ornaments, Joy and Noel, **198**, 211–212

Circle of birds table insert, **64**, 72
Cleaning of stitchery, 219
Clothing
  apron, blue-ribbon pickles, **143**, 146
  overalls
    boy's, with roller coaster motif, **140**, 148, 150
    girl's, with ice-cream cones, **140**, 150
  sweaters, cotton
    floral, **89**, 102
    flower basket, **111**, 114
  sweatshirts
    dinosaur and falling star inserts for, **178**, **179**, 184–185
    Halloween, **181**, 187
Colorfastness, testing for, 217
Correcting mistakes, 131, 219
Curtains, tulip, **71**, 77

D

"Decorate with Stitches" floss organizer, **88**, 102
Decorating-the-Christmas-tree wall hanging, **193**, 203–204
Dinosaur and falling star designs, sweatshirt inserts with, **178**, **179**, 184–185
Doily, rose, **42**, 54
Doll, Easter bunny, **85**, 92, 94, 96
Door sign, "baby sleeping," **154**, 159
Dresser jar, cherries insert for, **45**, 58

E

Easter baby bibs, **84**, 97
Easter bunny, **85**, 92, 94, 96
Errors, correcting, 131, 219

F

Falling star and dinosaur designs, sweatshirt inserts with, **178**, **179**, 184–185
Family scenes
  autumn, **12**, 20
  decorating-the-Christmas-tree, **193**, 203–204
  spring, **9**, 17
  summer, **10**, 18
  winter, **7**, 14

Farm blessing, **167,** 175
Fingertip towel, **121,** 133
Floral bellpull, **68,** 80, 82
Floral border sampler, **24,** 34
Floral purse, **89,** 100–101
Floral sweater, **89,** 102
Floral tablecloth, **118,** 131
Floral wall hanging, **116–117,** 123
Floss
    organizer for, "Decorate with
        Stitches," **88,** 102
    working with, 217
Flower basket border, **86,** 100
Flower basket cotton sweater, **111,** 114
Four-seasons sampler, **23,** 28, 34
Frame mats
    lily of the valley and primrose,
        118, 125
    Victorian roses, **41,** 54
Friendship sampler, **38,** 49

G

Garden sampler, **120,** 133
Gift bag, **121,** 133
Girl's overalls with ice-cream cones,
    140, 150
Guest towel, **121,** 133

H

Halloween sweatshirts, **181,** 187
Halloween treat bag, pumpkin, **180,**
    188–189
Hand towels, **118,** 131
Hearth stool, **66,** 74, 76
Heart pillow, Victorian roses, **41,** 54
Hearts sampler, **38,** 49
Heart wreath, rose, **43,** 56
Honesty sampler, **44,** 56

I

Ice-cream cones, girl's overalls with,
    140, 150

J

Jars
    dresser, cherries insert for, **45,** 58
    pickle, ribbon band for, **142,** 146
Jewelry boxes
    with monogram, **69,** 82
    pheasant, **164,** 171–172
    shamrock, **46,** 58, 61
Joy and Noel tree ornaments, **198,**
    211–212

K

Keepsake pillow, **108,** 112
Kite-flying family scene, **9,** 17

L

Liberty/freedom picnic basket, **138,** 144
Liberty/freedom sampler, **139,** 144,
    146
Lily of the valley and primrose mat,
    118, 125

M

Mary Montgomery sampler, **24,** 36
Materials, choosing, 217
Mats, picture frame
    lily of the valley and primrose,
        118, 125
    Victorian roses, **41,** 54
May basket, border for, **86,** 100
Maypole dance wall hanging, **87,** 97, 99
Merry Christmas pillow, **197,** 205, 208
Mini-samplers
    Christmas, **192, 194,** 204–205,
        209–210
    friendship and hearts, **38,** 49
Mirror with robin insert, **67,** 74
Mistakes, correcting, 131, 219
Monogram, jewelry box with, **69,** 82
Montgomery, Mary, sampler, **24,** 36

N

Napkin with wheat motif, **182,** 189
Nautical scenes
    "Adjust Our Sails," **91,** 106
    "Bless This Boat," **91,** 105
    porthole with sailboats, **90,** 106
Noel and Joy tree ornaments, **198,**
    211–212

O

Ornaments, Christmas tree, Joy and
    Noel, **198,** 211–212
Overalls
    boy's, with roller coaster motif, **140,**
        148, 150
    girl's, with ice-cream cones, **140,** 150

P–Q

Perforated paper, projects with
    flower basket border, **86,** 100
    mat, **41,** 54
    mini-samplers, **194,** 209–210
    place cards, **110,** 112
Pheasants
    blanket, **165,** 171–172
    jewelry box, **164,** 171–172
Photo album cover, "Welcome Guest,"
    39, 51
Photo mats
    lily of the valley and primrose,
        118, 125
    Victorian roses, **41,** 54
Pickle jar band, **142,** 146
Pickle recipe wall hanging, **142,** 146
Pickles, blue-ribbon, apron with,
    143, 146
Picnic basket, liberty/freedom,
    138, 144
Picture frame mats
    lily of the valley and primrose,
        118, 125
    Victorian roses, **41,** 54
Pictures
    A-plus teacher, **176,** 187
    porthole with sailboats, **90,** 106
    rose heart wreath, **43,** 56
    See also Family scenes; Samplers; Wall
        hangings

Pillows
 autumn, **162,** 169, 171
 birth announcement, **152,** 159
 heart-shaped, Victorian roses, **41,** 54
 Merry Christmas, **197,** 205, 208
 wedding keepsake, **108,** 112
Pine tree sampler, **199,** 212, 214
Place cards, **110,** 112
Place mats
 tulip, **70,** 77–78
 wheat, **182,** 189
Plate/tray, Santa treat, **196,** 210–211
Porthole with sailboats, **90,** 106
Primrose and lily of the valley mat, **118,** 125
Pumpkin treat bag, **180,** 188–189
Purse, floral, **89,** 100–101

R

Rabbit, Easter, **85,** 92, 94, 96
Recipe, pickle (wall hanging), **142,** 146
Ribbon band for jar, **142,** 146
Robin insert, mirror with, **67,** 74
Roller coaster motif, boy's overalls with, **140,** 148, 150
Rose doily, **42,** 54
Roses, Victorian, heart pillow and picture frame mat with, **41,** 54
Rose wreaths
 heart-shaped, **43,** 56
 tablecloth with, **119,** 131

S

Sachet, wedding, **110,** 112
Samplers
 birth, **153,** 156
 Christmas
  angels, **195,** 208–209
  mini-samplers, **192, 194,** 204–205, 209–210
  pine tree, **199,** 212, 214
 floral border, **24,** 34
 four-seasons, **23,** 28, 34
 friendship, **38,** 49
 garden, **120,** 133
 hearts, **38,** 49
 honesty, **44,** 56

Samplers (continued)
 liberty/freedom, **139,** 144, 146
 Mary Montgomery, **24,** 36
 schoolhouse, **177,** 187
 shamrock, **47,** 58
 state fair, **141,** 146, 148
 sunshine, **25,** 26
 wedding, **109,** 112
Sand-castle family scene, **10,** 18
Santa treat tray, **196,** 210–211
Schoolhouse sampler, **177,** 187
Scrapbook or photo album cover, "Welcome Guest," **39,** 51
Shamrock box, **46,** 58, 61
Shamrock sampler, **47,** 58
Shirts
 dinosaur and falling star insert for, **178, 179,** 184–185
 Halloween, **181,** 187
Snowman family scene, **7,** 14
Spring family scene, **9,** 17
State fair sampler, **141,** 146, 148
Stitch diagrams, 216
Stitching techniques, 218
Stool, hearth, **66,** 74, 76
Stuffed Easter bunny, **85,** 92, 94, 96
Summer family scene, **10,** 18
Sunshine sampler, **25,** 26
Sweaters, cotton
 floral, **89,** 102
 flower basket, **111,** 114
Sweatshirts
 dinosaur and falling star inserts for, **178, 179,** 184–185
 Halloween, **181,** 187

T–U

Tablecloths
 floral, **118,** 131
 rose wreath, **119,** 131
 Thanksgiving, **183,** 189
Table insert, circle of birds, **64,** 72
Teacher, A-plus, stitchery, **176,** 187
Thanksgiving table linens
 place mat and napkin, **182,** 189
 tablecloth, **183,** 189
Towels
 guest, **121,** 133
 hand, **118,** 131
Toy Easter bunny, **85,** 92, 94, 96
Tray, Santa treat, **196,** 210–211

Treat bag, pumpkin, **180,** 188–189
Tree ornaments, Joy and Noel, **198,** 211–212
Tulip curtains, **71,** 77
Tulip place mats, **70,** 77–78

V-Z

Valentine cards, **40**
Victorian roses heart pillow and picture frame mat, **41,** 54
Wall hangings
 "ABC's of Country," **166,** 175
 "Adjust Our Sails," **91,** 106
 "Bless This Boat," **91,** 105
 "Bless This Farm," **167,** 175
 "The Cat Did It," **45,** 61
 Christmas angels, **195,** 208–209
 decorating-the-Christmas-tree, **193,** 203–204
 floral, **116–117,** 123
 Maypole dance, **87,** 97, 99
 pickle recipe, **142,** 146
 See also Pictures; Samplers
Wedding items
 pillow, keepsake, **108,** 112
 place cards, **110,** 112
 sachet, **110,** 112
 sampler, **109,** 112
"Welcome Guest" book cover, **39,** 51
Winter family scene, **7,** 14
Wreaths of roses
 heart-shaped, **43,** 56
 tablecloth with, **119,** 131

Have BETTER HOMES AND GARDENS® magazine delivered to your door.
For information, write to:
MR. ROBERT AUSTIN
P.O. BOX 4536
DES MOINES, IA 50336